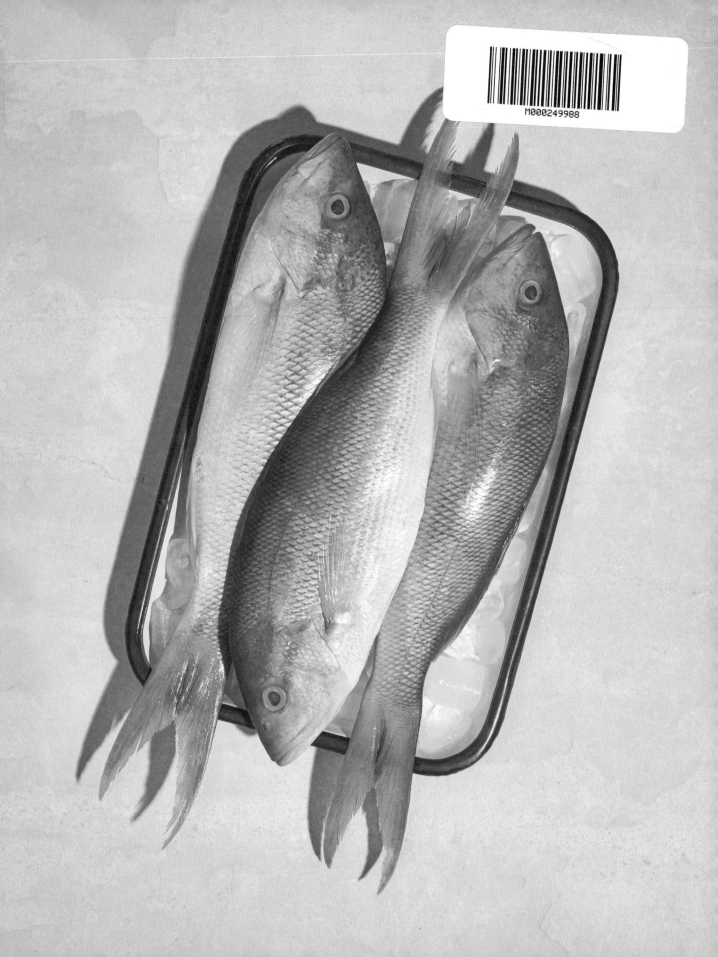

MIAMI COOKS

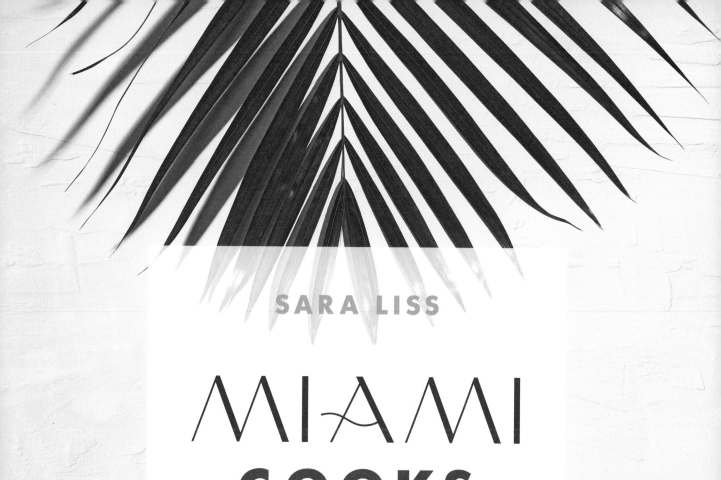

SARA LISS

MIAMI
COOKS

Recipes from the
City's Favorite Restaurants

Figure 1
Vancouver / Berkeley

To my husband, who understands that every project I take on will radiate into the rest of our family life and blessedly didn't flinch when I said I was writing this book. And to my kids, who are always up for a restaurant dine and at this point can probably critique a menu better than I can.

Cataloguing data are available from Library and Archives Canada
ISBN 978-1-77327-121-7 (hbk.)

Art direction and design by Naomi MacDougall
Photography by Michael Pisarri,
except p. 104: Groot Hospitality
Prop styling by Jocelyn Negron

Editing by Michelle Meade
Copy editing by Pam Robertson
Proofreading by Lucy Kenward
Indexing by Iva Cheung

Printed and bound in China by C&C Offset Printing Co., Ltd.
Distributed internationally by Publishers Group West

Figure 1 Publishing Inc.
Vancouver BC Canada
www.figure1publishing.com

RECIPE NOTES

All herbs are fresh unless stated otherwise.
Butter is unsalted unless stated otherwise.
Eggs are large unless stated otherwise.
Produce is always medium-sized unless stated otherwise.
Citrus juices are freshly squeezed.
Salt is kosher unless specified otherwise.
Pepper is always freshly ground.

CONTENTS

7 Foreword

8 Introduction

13 The Restaurants

14 The Recipes

174 Metric Conversion Chart

177 Acknowledgments

178 Index

184 About the Author

FOREWORD

BY ADEENA SUSSMAN

I've been coming to Miami to eat for a long time, and with each visit I eagerly anticipate the combination of newly minted hotspots and tried-and-true classics that await me.

As far as restaurant scenes go, Miami is in a league all its own. Not many cities in the United States—let alone the world—have what you can find here, and in such glorious abundance: superstar chefs who've made Miami their home (or second home); restaurants that celebrate multicultural cuisine, from Cubanos to quenelles and everything else the globe has to offer; diners as gorgeous as the food itself; and a confluence of talent, variety, and only-in-Miami showmanship that makes this town a singular dining destination.

But we all know that a great meal is about so much more than the food. As someone who reviewed eating establishments for years—and still eats out several times a week—I'm well aware that every restaurant is its own unique ecosystem, with a compelling story and a culinary vision that is as much about the people behind it as the food it sends out from the kitchen every night.

The human element of restaurants is something the author of this book, Sara Liss, understands better than most. An OG Miami food "influencer" before the term even existed, Sara is always rooting for chefs to succeed, and supporting them as they endeavor to bring something exciting and new to the Miami dining scene. I can't tell you how refreshing it is to sit down to a meal with someone who never seems jaded, only optimistic about her next bite.

She knows the cooks, their food, and everything that goes into creating a memorable experience for a diner.

But she also keeps it real. She knows that good food, good service, and good vibes aren't just fashioned out of whole cloth. She's the one sneaking back into the kitchen to high-five the pastry chef, and racing to her third lunch to make sure she's covered her P's and Q's, getting the scoop so you don't have to. She has the tea on who's cooking where, who's at the table next to you, and the dish you absolutely must. have. tonight.

Every year I look forward to the South Beach Wine and Food Festival for two main reasons: to reunite with the festival's founder, Lee Brian Schrager, with whom I've written two books, and the chance to hang out with Sara, whose excitement about her next meal is highly contagious. She has been my partner in crime for so many local restaurant adventures I've failed to keep count, and is one of my go-to sources for the ultimate question: where must I eat in Miami right now?

So I can think of no one better than Sara to write this book. It speaks to the deep relationships she has formed in the restaurant community, the admiration she has engendered from its chefs, her endless font of knowledge, and the way she celebrates the very best this town has to offer. And that is all reflected in these pages: a glorious assemblage of the evolving story of Miami dining, curated by Sara herself. Enjoy, knowing you are in very good hands and that reading these recipes will make you hungry…

7

INTRODUCTION

When it comes to food cities, it's time for Miami to hang with the grown-ups. No longer just a pretty place with flashy backdrops and ho-hum food, we're now home to James Beard–recognized chefs, a fistful of food halls, and the highest-grossing independent restaurant in the nation (hi, Joe's Stone Crab!).

But it wasn't always like this. Not many years ago Miami's food scene consisted of little more than Cuban diners, Jewish delis, and a few salty fish houses. Now, of course, we've got our share of celebrity chefs opening locations here, and some of our restaurants have even begun to expand beyond our borders. We are now a city brimming with culinary possibility and fame, and we're still learning how to manage it all.

In 2008, I was tapped to write and edit a daily magazine geared towards nightlife and dining, with the caveat that each day we had to cover something new, exciting, and heretofore undiscovered. The bulk of the stories focused on restaurants, obviously. "There's no way this will succeed," I remember thinking, panicking. "I will run out of openings!" After all, Miami isn't New York, Chicago, or Los Angeles—heck, it isn't even a poor man's Philly. We don't have the volume of new restaurants those cities have. We don't have the *talent*. Oh, was I wrong. That publication went strong for more than six years with each week's issue showcasing new and fascinating developments in our dining scene. I like to think we covered the new vanguard of

Miami dining with emerging talents like Brad Kilgore (page 64), Michael Beltran (page 22), and Michael Lewis (page 108) branching out on their own and opening multiple locations while honing their hospitality and culinary brands. Wynwood transformed from a gritty warehouse and gallery district to a restaurant haven, South Beach continued to attract the bulk of attention, and the Design District reinvented itself as a global destination for luxury and upscale dining.

Quirky things happened, too. Cesar Zapata and Aniece Meinhold's Phuc Yea (page 138) popped up in a sketchy downtown location on a shoestring budget. Bernie Matz (page 36) and Scott Linquist (page 50) initiated a taco renaissance by parlaying their experiences running major restaurants into creating taco joints that were both delicious and ridiculously fun. David Foulquier (page 78) took a chance on a neglected downtown space and blended his Persian heritage with Italian comfort food to create what he calls "feel good food." And Eileen Andrade (page 70), who saw a void in the hinterlands of Miami's suburbs, decided to make Korean noodles and Cuban fried rice for the West Kendall crowd. They repaid the kindness by lining up in droves for tables.

Miami is the perfect place for a self-starter. We lack the obstacles to advancement that so many other metropolitan cities seem to have. We're also very warm and welcoming—we can thank our Latin culture for that—and we're less judgmental than other towns that may foist food-snobbery

on earnest entrepreneurs. We love our food fresh and inventive, but we also like a good time. The hordes that drink rosé all day and dance to live DJs at Seaspice (page 156) may not realize it, but Chef Angel Leon is creating some of the most head-turning dishes this side of the Miami River. And while the crowds that pack Komodo (page 104) are coming for the nightlife-y feel of the "club-sterant," the kitchen churns out some of the best Peking duck in the city.

Of course, the simplest pleasures are the most rewarding. You can easily stroll down Lincoln Road during the day and stop for lunch at a patio café, and at night, head to Little Havana for rum cocktails, live jazz, and salsa dancing. You can find a great Cuban sandwich almost anywhere in the city, and you'll want to get your hands on as many stone crabs as possible, of course.

And while Miami is arguably the Cuban food capital of America, there are so many more ethnic cuisines available to diners willing to test their palates. Peruvian, Venezuelan, Puerto Rican, Haitian, Jamaican—the list goes on and on. And we've got a treasure trove of tropical fruit. Mangoes, papayas, starfruit, guava, and plantains are cheaper, more abundant, and *much* tastier in Miami than probably anywhere else in the country. It's fascinating to see the chefs in this book looking to these assorted traditions for inspiration and adaptation, using Miami's gorgeous produce to create a unique culinary language that's becoming emblematic of the city.

Chefs and restaurateurs take a big risk opening a restaurant anywhere, but in a place like Miami there's often more room to be adventurous, experiment, and evolve. We're lucky to have so many culinary stars in Miami taking these risks, and it's exciting to see some of them earn national recognition for their talent and hard work. Miami's food scene is ready to be taken seriously, and for proof of its undeniable progress, open these pages and dive in.

THE RESTAURANTS

16 27
JIMMY LEBRON

22 ARIETE
MICHAEL BELTRAN

26 BAR COLLINS
FREDERIC DELAIRE

30 BEAKER AND GRAY
BRIAN NASAJON

36 BODEGA TAQUERIA
Y TEQUILA
BERNIE MATZ

40 BOULUD SUD
DANIEL BOULUD

46 CECCONI'S
MIAMI BEACH
SERGIO SIGALA

50 COYO TACO
SCOTT LINQUIST

56 CRUST
**KLIME AND
ANITA KOVACESKI**

60 EDGE STEAK & BAR
**AARON BROOKS AND
HECTOR LLOMPART**

64 EMBER
BRAD KILGORE

70 FINKA TABLE & TAP
EILEEN ANDRADE

74 A FISH CALLED
AVALON
KAL ABDALLA

78 FOOQ'S
DAVID FOULQUIER

82 HAKKASAN
JIAN HENG (KENNY) LOO

86 JAYA AT THE
SETAI
VIJAYUDU VEENA

90 THE JIM
AND NEESIE
DANIEL ROY

94 JUVIA/
SUSHI GARAGE
SUNNY OH

98 KIKI ON
THE RIVER
STEVE RHEE

104 KOMODO
DAVID GRUTMAN

108 KYU
**STEVEN HAIGH AND
MICHAEL LEWIS**

114 LA MAR BY
GASTÓN ACURIO
DIEGO OKA

118 LEKU
MIKEL GOIKOLEA

122 LT STEAK &
SEAFOOD
LAURENT TOURONDEL

126 MALIBU FARM
MIAMI BEACH
HELENE HENDERSON

130 NIKKI BEACH
FRANK FERREIRO

134 OPEN KITCHEN
INES CHATTAS

138 PHUC YEA
**ANIECE MEINHOLD
AND CESAR ZAPATA**

144 RED, SOUTH
BEACH
PETER VAUTHY

148 SALUMERIA 104/
SPRIS
**ANGELO MASARIN AND
CARLO DONADONI**

152 SARDINIA
ENOTECA
RISTORANTE
**TONY GALLO AND
PIETRO VARDEU**

156 SEASPICE
ANGEL LEON

162 SHUCKERS
WATERFRONT BAR
AND GRILL
MIGUEL RIVERA

166 SOTTOSALE/
ESOTICO
**DANIELE DALLA POLA
AND IVO MAZZON**

170 VILLA AZUR
CARLOS TORRES

THE RECIPES

STARTERS AND LITTLE MEALS

62 Aussie Lamb Anticuchos with Baby Potatoes and Chile Sauce

47 Beef Tartare

143 Caramel Chicken Wings

168 Carne Salata e Rucola

171 Cauliflower Cakes

32 Cauliflower with Huancaina Sauce

163 Chilean Mussels

66 Cornbread with Short Rib Ragout

84 Crispy Spiced Prawns with Asian Pear and Almonds

115 Flor de Papa

153 Fregoletta

165 Garlic Shrimp

101 Grilled Octopus

19 Griot and Pikliz

120 Ham Croquetas

55 Mexican Street Corn *(Esquites)*

38 SoFla Fish Ceviche

34 Spanish Octopus

116 Tiradito Bachiche

103 Tuna Tartare

SALAD, SOUPS, AND SIDES

121 Beet Tartare Salad

92 Charred Romanesco with Celery Leaf Pesto and Harissa

123 Gruyère Popovers

136 Kale Caesar Salad with Crispy Pork Belly Lardons

24 Mamey Gazpacho

110 Roasted Cauliflower with Goat Cheese and Shishito-Herb Vinaigrette

132 Sexy Salad

145 Sweet Creamed Corn

BRUNCH

128 Avocado Pizza

27 Cubano "Croque Monsieur"

96 Hamachi Cilantro Rolls

150 Pizza Mortazza

58 Shrimp Cakes

MAINS

95 Chilean Sea Bass with Brown Butter–Soy Sauce

125 Cobia with Cara Cara Orange

146 Crab-Crusted Rib-Eye Steak

85 Crispy Orange Chicken

71 Cuban-Style Oxtail Stew

52 Duck Carnitas Tacos

39 Florida Fish Tacos

113 Florida Red Snapper

137 French Onion Risotto

87 Grilled Snapper with Tamarind Sauce

42 Harissa-Spiced Lamb, Eggplant, and M'Hamsa Couscous

72 Korean Braised Chicken with Glass Noodles

44 Lemon-Saffron Linguine

106 Maine Lobster

158 Market Fish Casserole

76 Orzo Seafood Paella

172 Pan-Roasted Scallops with Parsnip Purée and Braised Radishes

80 Persian Carrot and Sour Cherry Stew (Khoresh Havij Ba Aloo)

140 Pho Bo

23 Plantain Gnudi with Toasted Hazelnuts and Brown Butter

59 Seafood Risotto

133 Spaghetti aux Fruits de Mer

154 Spaghetti Bottarga

49 Spaghetti with Lobster

89 Thai Green Curry

20 Whole Fried Fish and Fixins

DESSERTS

29 Caramelized Strawberry Brioche

129 Grilled Chocolate Cake

77 Guiltless Lemon Soufflé Crepes

161 Lemon Mousse

63 Orelys Chocolate Namelaka with Coconut Crumble, Passionfruit Granite, and Banana Slices

81 Persian Gelato (Bastani)

151 Tiramisu

COCKTAILS

167 Esotico Rum Cup

107 Golden Geisha

93 Jim's Yellow Fedora

69 Rum Cake Mai Tai

Like so much of Miami, the food at 27 baffles and dazzles, marrying the various cultural and ethnic influences that make life here so dense and wonderful. It's a restaurant that I have a hard time describing when I recommend it to friends, which I often do.

"Is it Latin-inspired?" they'll ask.

"Well, yes… but there are also Caribbean influences," I'll add.

"It looks Middle Eastern," they'll say.

"It is. But you'll need to order an Indian dish and a few Italian ones," I'll suggest. *"Oh, and then there's the kimchi fried rice, which somehow makes sense."*

So yes, shrimp shumai will share space on the table with yogurt-tahini kale, chicken tagine, and Gabe's Arepa Platter. But before all of that, sip on a few cocktails and snack on tasty "tidbits" of Haitian *griot* (fried pork) and *pikliz* (pickled vegetable relish, page 19), and yucca fries.

The restaurant occupies and shares a thirties property with Freehand Miami, the high-end hostel where you can also find the award-winning bar Broken Shaker. Opened in 2014 by mixology gurus and Bar Lab partners Elad Zvi and Gabe Orta and designed by Roman and Williams, 27 feels like the hangout of your cool grandmother, replete with patterned wallpaper and vintage Israeli photos in antique frames.

During the annual South Beach Wine and Food Festival, the restaurant becomes a top-toque clubhouse where celeb chefs hobnob in the courtyard at after-hours parties or relax after the festival's closing event at 27's Sunday evening barbecue. One thing is for certain: this world-class destination celebrates local ingredients and fresh flavors by offering an inviting menu that champions native and international flavors, courtesy of Chef Jimmy LeBron.

DRESSING

1 cup orange juice

1 cup white vinegar

½ cup lemon juice

¼ cup lime juice

1 small Scotch bonnet
   or habanero pepper,
   chopped (see Note)

½ Tbsp salt

PIKLIZ

2 cups shredded cabbage

1 small carrot,
   coarsely grated

1 small onion, thinly sliced

2 Tbsp salt

2 cups Dressing (see here)

**EPIS (HAITIAN
SEASONING BASE)**

1 small yellow or Spanish
   onion, chopped (½ cup)

½ red bell pepper, seeded,
   deveined, and cut into
   ½-inch pieces

½ green bell pepper,
   seeded, deveined, and
   cut into ½-inch pieces

½ yellow bell pepper,
   seeded, deveined, and
   cut into ½-inch pieces

5 sprigs thyme, leaves
   only

½ cup chopped Italian
   parsley

½ cup chopped cilantro

6 cloves garlic,
   chopped

¼ cup salt

1 tsp ground cloves

1 cup lemon juice

PORK

5 lbs boneless pork
   shoulder, cut into
   4 equal pieces

Epis (see here, divided)

2 bay leaves

½ cup canola oil, plus
   extra if needed

ASSEMBLY

Parsley sprigs, for garnish

Griot and Pikliz

SERVES 6 TO 8 The classic Haitian dish pork *griot* (pronounced *gree-oh*) exemplifies Chef LeBron's deft hand for flavor: chunks of pork shoulder marinated in citrus, chiles, and spices are braised low and slow, then fried crisp and served alongside the tangy cabbage slaw *pikliz* (pronounced *pick-lees*). The slaw can be prepared in advance and stored in the refrigerator for up to five days.

DRESSING Combine all ingredients in a blender and purée until smooth.

PIKLIZ In a colander, combine cabbage, carrot, and onion. Sprinkle with salt and toss. Set aside for 30 minutes, then pat dry with paper towels.

In a bowl, toss together cabbage mixture and dressing and mix well. Store in an airtight container in the refrigerator for up to five days.

EPIS (HAITIAN SEASONING BASE) In a food processor, combine all ingredients and 2 cups water and process until smooth.

PORK In a 2-gallon ziptop bag or container, combine pork shoulder and 2 cups epis, ensuring the epis coats the pieces. Marinate for at least 1 hour, or preferably overnight.

Transfer pork to a stockpot and add bay leaves, remaining epis, and enough water to cover. Bring to a boil, then reduce heat to medium-low and simmer for 2½ to 3 hours, until meat is tender but not falling apart. Using a pair of tongs, transfer braised pork to a resting rack and set aside to cool. Refrigerate, uncovered, for 1 to 2 hours.

Cut pork into 3-inch pieces. Heat 1 inch of oil in a large shallow skillet over high heat. Working in batches, add pork and fry for 6 to 8 minutes on each side, until crispy.

ASSEMBLY Arrange pork griot on a serving platter and serve with pikliz. Garnish with parsley sprigs.

NOTE Scotch bonnets and habaneros are considered some of the hottest chiles in the world. Handle them with care by wearing gloves to avoid burns. And make sure to scrub clean your hands, knife, and any cutting boards that have touched the peppers.

PICKLED CARROTS

1 clove garlic

½ cup sugar

¼ cup salt

1 cup white vinegar

4 carrots, thinly sliced (2 cups)

SPICY TAHINI

6 Tbsp chopped canned chipotles in adobo

6 Tbsp white vinegar

2 Tbsp tahini

4 tsp roasted peanuts

4 tsp canola oil

1 tsp sugar

1 tsp salt

1 clove garlic

POBLANO-CUCUMBER ZHUG

1 seedless cucumber, finely chopped (1 cup)

1 poblano pepper, seeded and diced

2 cloves garlic, chopped

¼ cup chopped mint

¼ cup chopped cilantro

¼ cup chopped Italian parsley

2 Tbsp finely chopped shallots

2 Tbsp salt

Grated zest and juice of 2 oranges

1 cup extra-virgin olive oil

MANGO-CILANTRO ONIONS

2 mangoes, chopped (1½ cups)

½ large red onion, chopped (½ cup)

2 Tbsp chopped cilantro

Grated zest and juice of 2 limes

Whole Fried Fish and Fixins

SERVES 2 TO 4 This dish is a great way to jazz up a whole fish presentation. While the fish itself is fairly straightforward, the sauces take it to next-level status. What makes it extra fun is the ability to mix and match different flavors with the wonderful "fixins" and dips.

PICKLED CARROTS In a saucepan, combine garlic, sugar, salt, vinegar, and 2 cups water. Bring to a boil over medium-high heat. Reduce heat to medium-low and simmer for 5 minutes, stirring until sugar has dissolved.

Place carrots in a bowl and slowly pour in the hot pickling liquid. Set aside to cool completely to room temperature. Refrigerate for up to one month.

SPICY TAHINI In a food processor, blend all ingredients until smooth. Cover and store in the refrigerator until needed.

POBLANO-CUCUMBER ZHUG In a food processor, combine all ingredients except the oil and pulse until a coarse paste forms. Transfer mixture to a large bowl and whisk in oil. Cover and refrigerate until needed.

AVOCADO PICO

½ tomatillo, chopped

½ Hass avocado, chopped

½ red onion, finely chopped (½ cup)

½ red bell pepper, seeded, deveined, and finely chopped (½ cup)

¼ cup chopped cilantro

Juice of 2 limes

2 tsp salt

FISH

4 cups canola oil

1½ cups rice flour

1½ cups tapioca starch or cassava flour

1½ cups cornstarch

2 Tbsp paprika

2 Tbsp salt, plus extra for seasoning

1 (2- to 3-lb) whole snapper, skin on and filleted, pin bones removed, head and tail reserved

ASSEMBLY

6-inch tortillas, to serve

Lettuce leaves, to serve

MANGO-CILANTRO ONIONS Combine all ingredients in a bowl. Cover and refrigerate until needed.

AVOCADO PICO In a bowl, combine all ingredients and toss. Cover and refrigerate until needed.

FISH Heat oil in a deep fryer or deep saucepan over medium-high heat to 350°F.

In a shallow baking dish, combine flours, cornstarch, paprika, and salt. Cut fillets into 2-inch cubes and add to baking dish. Add head and tail and toss fish to coat evenly.

Working in batches, carefully lower fillet pieces into the oil and deep-fry for 7 to 8 minutes. Using a slotted spoon, transfer to a paper towel–lined plate to drain. Repeat with the head and tail. Lightly salt.

ASSEMBLY Array the fried fish pieces on a serving board and spoon the fixins into small bowls. Serve with tortillas and lettuce.

ARIETE

MICHAEL BELTRAN
owner and executive chef

"Where can we go for good Cuban food?" is a question I often get asked. And in 2016 a new contender was born: Ariete. Unlike the chintzy cafeteria-style diners that dish up overpriced rice and beans and fried plantains to busloads of tourists, this neighborhood spot in Coconut Grove showcases the kind of innovative Latin food our city is capable of. And there's nary a bowl of black beans on the menu.

Michael Beltran wasn't exactly a household name when he opened Ariete (the name alludes to his grandparents' restaurant in Pinar del Río, Cuba), but he certainly wasn't new to the game. His farm-focused culinary experience came courtesy of The Cypress Room, working under Chef Michael Schwartz, and at downtown's Tuyo with the godfather of Miami cooking, Norman Van Aken. And even before that, working his way up from bartender to line cook at Casa Juancho in Little Havana.

"Ariete is a reflection of Miami," says Beltran. "It's Cuban-inspired, American-influenced cooking concocted in the 305." And it's hyper local, with Beltran visiting Homestead farms and purveyors to inspire his daily specials. Patrons still swoon over his foie gras with sour orange and caramel plantains and cocoa nibs, years after it debuted on the opening night menu, while the chilled mamey soup (page 24) is a Miami take on classic gazpacho.

Beltran's Ark Hospitality Group is responsible for concepts such as Chug's (a Cuban diner), the South Beach bar The ScapeGoat, and Leña at Time Out Market, but Ariete remains the flagship. And all thanks to Beltran. That a chef who started out as a busser and dishwasher at a chain restaurant can now helm a mini-empire is a Miami success story. And we are all the better for it.

LEMON BROWN BUTTER

½ cup (1 stick) butter

Pinch of salt

1 Tbsp chopped lemon
(see Note)

1 tsp grated lemon zest

**CARAMELIZED
PLANTAINS**

1 Tbsp butter

3 plantains, sliced

PLANTAIN GNUDI

16 oz ricotta

1 egg

1 egg yolk

½ cup grated Parmesan

1 tsp black pepper

½ tsp salt

Caramelized Plantains
(see here, divided)

½ cup all-purpose flour

ASSEMBLY

2 Tbsp Lemon Brown
Butter (see here)

¼ cup toasted hazelnuts

Lemon balm leaves,
chopped

½ lemon

Plantain Gnudi with Toasted Hazelnuts and Brown Butter

SERVES 2 TO 4 Gnudi is a ricotta-based Italian dumpling that is lighter and airier than its denser cousin, the gnocchi. This simple yet elegant version is brought to life with the unlikely inclusion of caramelized plantains and is served with crunchy toasted hazelnuts and a zesty brown butter. Truly, it's nothing short of impressive.

LEMON BROWN BUTTER Combine butter and salt in a small saucepan and cook for 5 minutes on medium-low heat, until nutty brown. Transfer butter to a bowl and place in a larger bowl of ice water. Stir frequently for 5 minutes, until the edges solidify. Remove bowl from the ice water and gently beat with a wooden spoon until the butter is pale and creamy. Fold in chopped lemon and lemon zest. Set aside.

NOTE To make chopped lemon, remove skin and bitter white pith. Cut between the membranes to release the segments, then chop.

CARAMELIZED PLANTAINS Melt butter in a large frying pan over medium heat. Add plantains, then toss to coat. Cook for 5 minutes on each side, until tender and caramelized. Set aside.

PLANTAIN GNUDI In a medium bowl, combine ricotta, egg, and egg yolk and mix well. Stir in Parmesan, pepper, salt, and half of the caramelized plantains (reserve the rest). Sift in flour while stirring. Cover with plastic wrap and refrigerate for 2 hours.

Bring a saucepan of salted water to a boil. Using an ice-cream scoop, scoop out dough into individual dumplings. Lower dumplings into water, in batches of four, and cook for 4 to 5 minutes, until they rise to the surface. Transfer to a paper towel–lined plate and repeat with remaining gnudi.

ASSEMBLY Place warm dumplings in a shallow bowl and top with lemon brown butter, toasted hazelnuts, and the remaining caramelized plantains. Garnish with lemon balm and a squeeze of lemon juice.

GAZPACHO

1 lb beets

¼ cup extra-virgin olive oil, plus extra for drizzling and finishing

1 small onion, cut into matchstick slices (½ cup)

1 red bell pepper, seeded, deveined, and cut into matchstick slices

1½ lbs ripe mamey, peeled and seeded

1 clove garlic, sliced

½ cup red wine vinegar

Salt, to taste

Baby beet greens, for garnish

FETA CREAM

1 cup plain Greek yogurt

1 cup whey or milk

¾ cup feta cheese

½ cup crème fraîche

1 Tbsp coarse salt

Mamey Gazpacho

SERVES 2 TO 4 Tropical mamey fruit has a texture akin to a sweet potato, and its creamy, caramel sweetness adds depth to this refreshing soup. This orange-colored fruit is widely grown and sold in Cuba and on other islands in the Caribbean but we Miamians can find it easily at our local grocer. It is also Beltran's favorite fruit, so much so that he has a tattoo of it on his left arm. Served chilled, this first course makes a perfectly light and balanced starter.

GAZPACHO Preheat oven to 400°F. Place beets on a large sheet of aluminum foil, then drizzle with oil and wrap up to seal. Transfer to a baking sheet and roast for 1 hour. Set aside to cool, then peel. Chop one beet for garnish and reserve in the refrigerator until needed.

Heat the ¼ cup oil in a medium skillet over medium heat. Add onion and red pepper and sauté for 7 minutes, or until softened. Add beets and enough water to cover and bring to a boil over high heat. Boil for 5 minutes, until ingredients are softened.

Working in batches, transfer mixture to a blender and purée. Gradually add the mamey, garlic, and vinegar and blend until smooth. Season to taste with salt, then chill for at least 2 hours before serving.

FETA CREAM In a bowl, combine all ingredients and mix well.

ASSEMBLY Spoon gazpacho into bowls and top each serving with a dollop of feta cream. Top with the reserved chopped beets and beet greens and finish with a drizzle of olive oil.

BAR COLLINS

FREDERIC DELAIRE
executive chef

Chef Frederic Delaire is one of the only people in Miami who has fed a room of James Beard award winners in a single sitting. You see, the Loews Miami Beach Hotel is ground zero for the South Beach Wine and Food Festival, its visiting chefs, and its marquee event, the Saturday night tribute dinner—and as executive chef, Delaire has the Herculean task of leading his team to prep and plate a 500-person seated dinner consisting of five courses for the likes of José Andrés and Martha Stewart. "It's five days of culinary madness!" laughs Delaire about the week leading up to the dinner. "But it is always an honor and privilege to cook and help so many chefs that attend the festival," he adds.

Born and raised in France, Delaire fondly remembers summer vacations in his grand-parents' kitchen using old kitchen tools and perusing well-worn cookbooks. That curiosity eventually led to a stint working for culinary legend Alain Ducasse at Le Jules Verne in the Eiffel Tower and at the three-Michelin-star restaurant L'Aubergade.

Admirably resolute, the classically trained Delaire takes his tasks in stride, leading teams of hundreds to execute dinners at the hotel as well as overseeing all culinary operations from room service to the pool bar.

And when it came to designing the menu for the hotel's cushy-yet-busy lobby bar, Delaire looked to South Florida's mix of cultures and culinary traditions. "Bar Collins is a global menu inspired by Latin influence and local dishes," says Delaire. Everything from churrasco steak to the Cuban croque monsieur (page 27) is designed to comfort and welcome travelers who make the Loews their temporary home during their visit. And we can't think of a better person to welcome them.

PORK ROAST MARINADE

4 cloves garlic

2 tsp ground cumin

2 tsp salt

1 tsp dried oregano

½ tsp black pepper

1 cup orange juice

Juice of 2 lemons

Juice of 2 limes

2 Tbsp extra-virgin
olive oil

CUBAN-STYLE PORK ROAST

4 lbs pork shoulder, tied
like a loin (ask your
butcher)

1½ cups Pork Roast
Marinade (see here)

BÉCHAMEL SAUCE

3 Tbsp butter

¼ cup all-purpose flour

Pinch of nutmeg

Pinch of salt

4 cups milk

1 cup grated Gruyère

CUBAN MAYO

½ cup mayonnaise

½ cup Dijon mustard

ASSEMBLY

8 slices brioche loaf
or country bread,
½-inch thick (divided)

2 cups Béchamel Sauce
(see here)

16 thin slices Cuban-Style
Pork Roast (see here)

16 slices cooked ham

1 cup Cuban Mayo
(see here)

4 large pickles,
thinly sliced

16 slices Swiss cheese

1 cup grated Gruyère

Cubano "Croque Monsieur"

SERVES 4 A Cuban play on a French classic, this towering sandwich teems with slow-roasted pork, an indulgent béchamel sauce, and many layers of ham and Swiss. You'll need a day in advance to marinate the pork, but trust me, this hearty and satisfying meal is well worth it, especially when it's followed by a strong Cuban coffee.

PORK ROAST MARINADE In small food processor, combine garlic, cumin, salt, oregano, and pepper. (Alternatively, use a pestle and mortar.) Transfer paste to a small bowl, then whisk in citrus juices and oil.

CUBAN-STYLE PORK ROAST Place pork in a large ziptop bag or container and pour in marinade. Rub marinade over the entire pork shoulder and refrigerate for 24 hours.

Preheat oven to 325°F. Transfer pork and marinade to a roasting pan and roast for 2½ hours, basting occasionally, until the center is tender and the internal temperature reaches 145°F. Set aside to rest at room temperature for 20 minutes, then refrigerate.

BÉCHAMEL SAUCE Melt butter in a medium saucepan over medium heat. Add flour, nutmeg, and salt and stir for 2 to 3 minutes, until golden. Pour in milk and whisk continuously for 6 minutes, until sauce has thickened. Remove from heat and stir in cheese, until melted and combined. Set aside.

CUBAN MAYO In a small bowl, combine mayo and mustard. Set aside.

ASSEMBLY Preheat oven to 420°F.

Place 4 slices of brioche (or country bread) on a baking sheet. Add a layer of béchamel sauce, then 2 slices pork and 2 slices ham. Add a thin layer of Cuban mayo and sliced pickles. Add 2 slices of Swiss cheese. Then repeat layers. Cover with the remaining 4 slices of bread. Using the palm of your hand, gently press on the sandwiches to compact.

Spread a generous layer of béchamel on top of the last piece of bread and top with Gruyère. Bake for 10 to 12 minutes, until the tops of the sandwiches are golden brown. Transfer to plates and serve.

PASTRY CREAM

½ cup sugar

5 egg yolks

¼ cup cornstarch

2 cups whole milk

2 Tbsp butter, at room temperature

½ vanilla bean, halved lengthwise

STRAWBERRY SAUCE

1 cup strawberries, halved

½ cup sugar

1 Tbsp lemon juice

CARAMELIZED BRIOCHE

1 cup (2 sticks) butter

1 cup sugar

1 loaf brioche, cut into 4 (1-inch-thick) pieces

STRAWBERRY SALAD

2 cups strawberries, halved

1 Tbsp chopped mint

ASSEMBLY

2 cups Pastry Cream (see here)

½ cup whipped cream

1 tsp Grand Marnier (optional)

4 slices Caramelized Brioche (see here)

1 cup Strawberry Sauce (see here)

Strawberry Salad (see here)

Caramelized Strawberry Brioche

SERVES 4 This sexy little dessert is Bar Collins's secret weapon. A rich pastry cream laced with Grand Marnier is smothered over a decadent slice of caramelized brioche and then topped with a minted strawberry salad and a drizzle of strawberry sauce. Pair it with a strong espresso for a decadent brunch dish or a hearty dessert.

PASTRY CREAM In a bowl, whisk together sugar, egg yolks, and cornstarch.

Combine milk and butter in a saucepan over medium heat. Scrape the vanilla seeds into the pan and whisk in. Bring to a boil, then remove pan from heat and set aside for 10 minutes.

Pour the vanilla-infused milk into the egg-cornstarch mixture and whisk continuously for 10 seconds. Pour the mixture back into the saucepan and bring to a boil over medium heat. Boil for 1 minute, whisking the entire time, until thickened. Pour the pastry cream into a bowl. Set aside to cool, then refrigerate.

STRAWBERRY SAUCE In a medium saucepan, combine strawberries, sugar, and lemon juice and bring to a boil over medium-high heat. Cook for 2 to 3 minutes, until strawberries have softened. Transfer to a blender and purée until smooth. Refrigerate until needed.

CARAMELIZED BRIOCHE Melt butter in a skillet over low heat. Add sugar and cook for 8 to 10 minutes, until caramel-like. Remove from heat and dip the 4 slices of brioche into the caramel, coating both sides. Place the slices on a nonstick surface and set aside to cool for 15 minutes, until brioche is slightly crispy.

STRAWBERRY SALAD In a bowl, combine strawberries and mint. Cover and refrigerate until needed.

ASSEMBLY In a bowl, whisk together pastry cream, whipped cream, and Grand Marnier, if using. Place the slices of caramelized brioche on plates and spread the cream over the surface, about ½ inch thick. Arrange the strawberry salad on top, then dot strawberry sauce and around the plates.

BEAKER AND GRAY

BRIAN NASAJON
owner and executive chef

We can all thank the philosophy department at New York University for Beaker and Gray. Because if it weren't for Brian Nasajon's pivot from that academic pursuit to train at Josh Capon's Lure Fishbar in Manhattan, we wouldn't have this incredibly delicious restaurant in our midst.

That job at Lure eventually led Nasajon to opportunities in many more kitchens— including helming both SushiSamba locations here in his native Miami, which spurred him to open his own place. In 2016, Nasajon joined forces with friend and cocktail master Ben Potts to create this ambitious spot, converting an old ice factory in Wynwood into a cozy cavern offering shareable small plates and serious cocktails. Exposed brick walls, wood beam ceilings, and the open kitchen make the place feel current and urbane yet also warm and welcoming—it's perfect for a date or for happy hour with friends.

And while most chefs and restaurants favor one school of thinking and eating over another, Nasajon is unusually ambidextrous, as comfortable whipping up ethereal foams as he is expertly frying cheeseburger croquettes. With influences from Asia, Europe, and South America, the dishes at Beaker and Gray upend convention while remaining true to the integrity of the ingredients. This is apparent in dishes such as the cauliflower topped with a mélange of *huancaina* sauce, bacon, and a yuzu foam (page 32) and Nasajon's pastrami *medianoche* sandwich, which plays with a Miami culinary trope and pays homage to his Jewish heritage. Every meal at Beaker and Gray is exciting, satisfying, and surprising—which is why we return time and again.

FACING Cauliflower with Huancaina Sauce

HUANCAINA SAUCE

2 Tbsp vegetable oil

4 shallots, chopped (½ cup)

6 cloves garlic, chopped

¼ cup aji amarillo paste

1 Tbsp salt

½ cup sake

2 cups heavy cream

¼ cup grated Parmesan

BACON VINAIGRETTE

3 cloves garlic, chopped

2 Tbsp chopped Fresno pepper, with seeds

1 Tbsp chopped jalapeño, with seeds

¾ cup sugar (divided)

1½ Tbsp salt (divided)

1 cup white vinegar

12 slices bacon, cut into ¼-inch pieces (2 cups)

Cauliflower with Huancaina Sauce

SERVES 6 TO 8 *Huancaina* sauce is a spicy Peruvian cheese sauce usually served over boiled potatoes, but for this dish Brian Nasajon replaces the potatoes with roasted cauliflower smothered in the sauce and adds a bacon vinaigrette for a smoky punch. The sauce is enhanced with *aji amarillo,* an orange chile native to South America. Look for jars of bright orange *aji amarillo* paste at your local market.

HUANCAINA SAUCE Heat oil in a skillet over medium-high heat. Add shallots and garlic and sauté for 4 minutes, until slightly translucent. Add aji amarillo paste and salt and cook for 5 minutes, stirring frequently. Add sake and cook for another 5 minutes, until reduced by three-quarters. Stir in cream, then reduce heat to medium and cook for another 10 minutes. Remove from heat, add Parmesan and blend sauce with an immersion blender until it has the consistency of thin yogurt.

BACON VINAIGRETTE Combine garlic, peppers, ½ cup sugar, 1 tablespoon salt, and the vinegar in a small saucepan and bring to a boil. Turn off heat and set aside to cool to room temperature. Transfer to a blender and process vinaigrette until smooth.

Heat a large skillet on medium-high heat. Add bacon and cook for 6 minutes, until browned and crisp. Add remaining ¼ cup sugar and ½ tablespoon salt and stir for 1 minute. Pour in 1½ cups vinaigrette and cook for another 5 to 7 minutes, until mixture has reduced by a quarter. Set aside to cool.

YUZU FOAM BASE

1 cup yuzu juice

1 tsp soy lecithin (see Note)

CAULIFLOWER

¼ cup vegetable oil

3 lbs multicolored cauliflower florets

Huancaina Sauce (see here)

½ cup Bacon Vinaigrette (see here)

ASSEMBLY

Yuzu Foam Base (see here)

¼ cup queso fresco, crumbled

Bunch of scallions, chopped

YUZU FOAM BASE Combine yuzu juice, soy lecithin, and ½ cup water in a small saucepan and cook over medium heat for 5 minutes, or until soy lecithin is dissolved. Bring to a simmer, then remove from heat. Using an immersion blender, mix for 3 minutes, until yuzu liquid is completely blended. Place the saucepan in an ice bath and set aside to cool.

NOTE Lecithin—a food additive that can come from various sources, including soy—is often used as an emulsifier. Soy lecithin can be purchased online.

CAULIFLOWER Heat oil in a large skillet over medium heat. Add florets and cook for 20 minutes, until lightly charred. (If needed, finish the cauliflower by broiling them in the oven for 2 minutes.)

Add enough huancaina sauce to the skillet to fully cover the cauliflower, then add bacon vinaigrette and sauté on low heat for 3 minutes, until warmed through.

ASSEMBLY Using an immersion blender, turn yuzu liquid into a foam.

Arrange cauliflower florets on a large serving platter and top with queso fresco and scallions. Garnish with a few spoonfuls of yuzu foam and serve.

OCTOPUS

5 lbs octopus tentacles

2 bay leaves

5 black peppercorns

COCONUT-CILANTRO SAUCE

2 jalapeño peppers, seeded

½ cup sugar

¼ cup candied ginger

2 Tbsp sweet coconut flakes

2 Tbsp salt

3 cups coconut milk

¼ cup lemon juice

¼ cup lime juice

1 Tbsp Sriracha

½ cup chopped cilantro

CHILE-VINAIGRETTE AIOLI

3 cloves garlic, chopped

½ cup sugar

2 Tbsp salt, plus extra to taste

2 Tbsp chopped Fresno pepper

2 Tbsp chopped shallots

1 Tbsp chopped jalapeño

1 cup champagne vinegar

¼ cup red wine vinegar

2 Tbsp fish sauce

1 cup mayonnaise

INFUSED WATERMELON

1 cup lime juice

1 cup lemon juice

2 dried Thai chiles

1 Tbsp chopped basil

¼ large seedless watermelon, peeled and sliced into 1-inch cubes

Spanish Octopus

SERVES 8 TO 10 There are many components to this octopus dish, but a few, including the vinaigrette and the coconut sauce, can be prepared in advance. And once it all comes together, this showstopper will impress even the most discerning dinner guests.

OCTOPUS Preheat oven to 300°F.

In a deep baking pan, combine octopus, bay leaves, and peppercorns. Add enough water to cover and seal pan with aluminum foil. Cook for 3 hours, until tender. Transfer octopus to a baking sheet and refrigerate until cooled.

COCONUT-CILANTRO SAUCE In a medium saucepan, combine all ingredients except the cilantro and bring to a boil over high heat. Turn off heat and set aside to cool completely.

Add cilantro. Using an immersion blender, blend mixture until smooth. Cover and refrigerate until needed.

CHILE-VINAIGRETTE AIOLI In a small saucepan, combine all ingredients except fish sauce and mayonnaise and bring to a boil. Remove pan from the heat, stir in fish sauce, and set aside to cool.

Transfer the mixture to a food processor and purée until smooth. Combine 1 cup vinaigrette and the mayo in a bowl, then season with salt to taste. Cover and refrigerate until needed.

INFUSED WATERMELON In a small saucepan, combine all ingredients except for the watermelon and bring to a boil. Remove from heat. Using an immersion blender, blend until smooth. Set aside to cool.

Transfer watermelon to a baking dish or large ziptop bag. Pour in the liquid and soak for 15 minutes. Remove watermelon and set aside until needed.

HEARTS OF PALM

½ lb fresh hearts of palm, sliced into ½-inch-thick disks

1 Tbsp canola oil

1 tsp salt

POTATO CRISPS

2 Yukon Gold potatoes, peeled and thinly sliced using a mandoline

1 cup canola oil

1 tsp salt

ASSEMBLY

2 Tbsp canola oil

Octopus (see here)

2 scallions, sliced

1 cup Chile-Vinaigrette Aioli (see here)

HEARTS OF PALM In a bowl, combine hearts of palm, oil, and salt and gently toss.

Heat a skillet over medium-high heat. Add hearts of palm and carefully char for 2 minutes on each side. Remove and set aside to cool.

POTATO CRISPS Place potatoes in a bowl of cold water and rinse to extract starch. Repeat if needed, then dry the slices before frying.

Heat oil in a large skillet over high heat. Add potatoes and fry for 8 minutes, until golden brown. Transfer to a paper towel–lined plate and season with salt.

ASSEMBLY Heat oil in a large skillet over high heat. Add octopus and char for 5 to 7 minutes on each side. Remove and set aside to cool, then slice tentacles into 1-inch pieces.

In a bowl, combine octopus, scallions, and chile-vinaigrette aioli.

Pour a pool of coconut-cilantro sauce onto a deep serving platter. Arrange pieces of octopus on the sauce and top with hearts of palm and watermelon. Garnish with potato crisps.

BODEGA TAQUERIA Y TEQUILA

BERNIE MATZ
executive chef

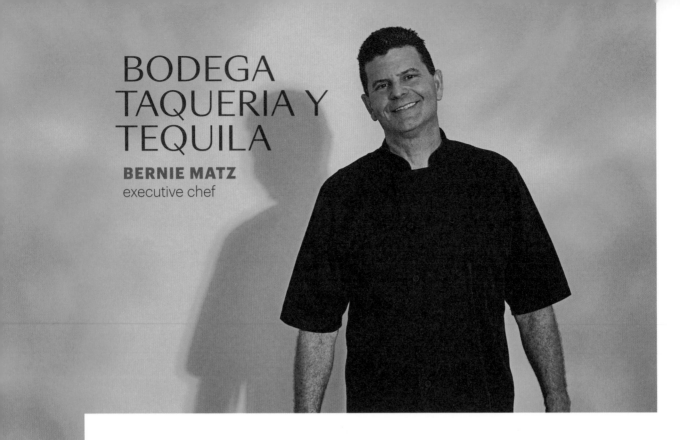

Bodega is where partygoers and clubbers end their nights in South Beach. The taco stand with a hidden lounge has become known as the place to cure or prolong hedonistic nights out depending on what you're up for. Opened by a cadre of hospitality pros with a love of Mexican food and tequila cocktails, this cavernous covert club occupies a former auto garage that is accessed via a smaller counter-service taqueria off Alton Road. Enter through either a meat locker door or the one from a porta-potty and behold a two-story lounge and bar tricked out with brick walls, Edison bulbs, cheeky neon signs, velvet couches, and a DJ booth.

But despite the nightlife trappings, the tacos have a gourmet pedigree thanks to Chef Bernie Matz, the Miami food scene veteran who brought us popular South Beach spots The Café at Books & Books and Bernie's L.A. Café. In 2014, he became executive director of culinary operations for Menin Hospitality, overseeing and adding his personal touch to all the restaurant outlets. Inspired by small roadside spots on the outskirts of Mexico City, the focus at Bodega is on flame-broiled meat cooked low and slow on rotating spits.

"The humble taco would be beneath most chefs until you begin to understand the complexity that goes into it," says Matz. "I was excited to dive deep into Mexican cuisine for this project. I've also explored different layers of heat and textures while creating this menu."

With a four a.m. closing time, every night is packed with West Avenue condo dwellers, local food bloggers, and lucky tourists, noshing on staples such as tacos al pastor topped with charred pineapple and *salsa rosada* (page 39) or grilled rib-eye burritos stuffed with rice, black beans, and chile crema. All of which are sure to prevent a hangover—or so one might hope.

FACING SoFla Fish Ceviche and Florida Fish Tacos

MARINATED FISH

2 lbs grouper fillets, pin bones removed

Juice of 5 limes (1 cup)

½ tsp sea salt

CEVICHE

1 jalapeño, seeded and finely chopped

1 tomato, chopped

1 small red onion, chopped

½ green bell pepper, seeded, deveined, and chopped

½ cup chopped cilantro

¼ tsp sea salt

¼ tsp sugar

⅛ tsp black pepper

Juice of 1 lime

Marinated Fish (see here)

½ red cabbage, shredded

1 avocado, thinly sliced, for garnish (optional)

1 Tbsp finely chopped cilantro, for garnish

SoFla Fish Ceviche

SERVES 6 TO 8 This traditional Peruvian dish is given a Mexican spin with cilantro and a little sugar and makes for an easy and refreshing starter to a casual lunch. Chef Bernie Matz prefers grouper but a local white fish such as snapper or corvina would work just as well.

MARINATED FISH Rinse fish under cold running water, then cut into ½-inch cubes. Place in a glass bowl.

In another bowl, whisk together lime juice and salt. Pour mixture into the glass bowl (just enough to cover the fish). Cover and refrigerate for 1 hour.

CEVICHE Combine all ingredients except the marinated fish and the garnishes in a large bowl.

Drain fish, gently squeezing each piece to remove any excess liquid, and then add it to the ceviche mixture. Gently toss to mix, then cover and refrigerate until ready to serve.

Arrange the cabbage on a platter, set the chilled ceviche on top, and garnish with avocado slices, if using, and chopped cilantro.

SALSA ROSADA

1 cup Mexican crema or sour cream (see Note)

1 cup mayonnaise

½ cup Sriracha

Juice of ½ lime

Salt and black pepper, to taste

MANGO PICO DE GALLO

1 mango, peeled and cut into a ½-inch dice

1 tomato, chopped

1 red onion, finely chopped

1 jalapeño, seeded and finely chopped

½ bunch cilantro, chopped

2 Tbsp extra-virgin olive oil

1 Tbsp chili powder

Juice of 1 lime

Salt and black pepper, to taste

PANKO-BREADED FISH

½ cup vegetable oil

2 cups all-purpose flour

3 eggs, lightly beaten

2 cups panko breadcrumbs

2 lbs skinless grouper, mahi mahi, snapper, or tilapia fillets, cut into 1½-inch chunks

Salt and black pepper, to taste

ASSEMBLY

Vegetable oil, for deep-frying

1 cup frozen shredded hash browns

Sea salt, to taste

Cilantro, to serve

Lime wedges, to serve

Warm 6-inch corn tortillas, to serve

Florida Fish Tacos

SERVES 6 TO 8 The making of a great fish taco requires two things: fresh fish and great crunch. These tacos are exceptional because Chef Bernie Matz adds an additional element of crunch with potato sticks.

SALSA ROSADA In a bowl, combine all ingredients. Refrigerate until needed.

MANGO PICO DE GALLO In a large bowl, combine all ingredients and toss lightly. Refrigerate until needed.

NOTE Mexican crema is a thinner and less sour version of sour cream. It can be found in ethnic supermarkets.

PANKO-BREADED FISH Heat oil in a skillet over high heat. Place flour in a shallow dish. Combine eggs and ¼ cup water in a separate shallow dish and place breadcrumbs in another. Season fish with salt and pepper.

Dredge fish in flour, then egg mixture and breadcrumbs. Add fish to pan, working in batches to prevent overcrowding, and fry for 3 minutes on each side, until golden. Using a slotted spoon, transfer fish to a paper towel–lined plate and season with salt. Keep warm.

ASSEMBLY Heat oil to 350°F in a deep fryer or deep saucepan over medium-high heat. Carefully lower hash browns into the oil and deep-fry for 3 to 4 minutes. Using a slotted spoon, transfer hash browns to a paper towel–lined plate. Set aside to cool slightly, then crumble and sprinkle with salt.

Arrange fish on a serving platter and put the salsa rosada, mango pico de gallo, and crumbled hash browns in bowls. Serve family-style with cilantro, limes, and tortillas.

BOULUD SUD

DANIEL BOULUD
executive chef

Daniel Boulud requires no introduction. His restaurants span the globe—from Singapore to Boston to his eponymous two-Michelin-starred restaurant in New York City—and have earned countless accolades, including three James Beard awards. So when this highly acclaimed French chef and restaurateur opened an outpost in our humble city over a decade ago, food lovers rejoiced. First launched as db Bistro Moderne, the restaurant was transformed in 2018 into the Mediterranean-style Boulud Sud.

It's a plush downtown spot infused with a worldly charm that sets it apart from other hotel dining rooms. The multi-room eatery on the ground floor of the sleek JW Marriott Marquis has a decidedly polished bohemian vibe with lush plants, free-flowing olive oil decanters, linen seating, Moroccan-inspired tile floors, and original artwork by artist Vik Muniz.

Dining at Boulud Sud is a passport to the Mediterranean, one that transports you to far-flung countries without ever having to leave downtown Miami. An evening meal might include crispy artichokes *alla Romana*, a Moroccan summer tagine, or the lemon-saffron linguine (page 44). There's an emphasis on grilled fish and lamb, as well as an abundance of fresh vegetables, but what gets us every time is the complimentary basket of madeleines at the end of the meal. Each one is a warm, lemon-scented hug: equally sweet and comforting.

FACING Harissa-Spiced Lamb, Eggplant, and M'Hamsa Couscous

HARISSA SPICE MIX

½ cup harissa powder

½ cup garlic powder

3 Tbsp dried parsley

2 Tbsp dried mint

2 Tbsp ground coriander

LAMB

5 tsp Harissa Spice Mix
(see here)

¼ cup grapeseed oil

1 (3-lb) lamb saddle,
cut into 2 loins and
2 tenderloins

½ tsp dried mint

½ tsp dried parsley

EGGPLANT PURÉE

½ cup extra-virgin olive oil
(divided)

2 large eggplants, halved
lengthwise

Salt and white pepper,
to taste

1 shallot, sliced

2 cloves garlic, sliced

1 tsp Harissa Spice Mix
(see here)

Juice of 1 lemon

GLAZED EGGPLANT

2 large eggplants, cut
lengthwise into ½-inch-
thick slices

1 tsp salt

1 tsp black pepper

¼ cup extra-virgin olive oil

¼ cup sherry vinegar

2 Tbsp honey

Harissa-Spiced Lamb, Eggplant, and M'Hamsa Couscous

SERVES 8 Harissa is a North African chili paste and an essential condiment for Tunisian cuisine. Chef Boulud uses it throughout this dish to bring out the bold flavors of the lamb, season a bright eggplant purée, and enliven nutty couscous. Make sure to allow enough time to marinate the lamb a day in advance.

HARISSA SPICE MIX Combine all the spices in a small container.

LAMB In a small bowl, combine harissa spice mix and oil. Brush mixture onto the lamb and then sprinkle with mint and parsley. Place lamb in a ziptop bag or container and refrigerate overnight.

EGGPLANT PURÉE Preheat oven to 350°F.

Brush oil over eggplants, then sprinkle with salt and pepper. Transfer to a baking sheet, cut-side down, and bake for 25 minutes, or until very tender. Remove from the oven and set aside to cool. Scrape away the flesh and discard the skin.

Heat a ¼-inch layer of oil in a large skillet over medium heat. Add shallot and garlic and sauté for 2 minutes, until translucent. Add eggplant and spice mix and cook for another 5 minutes, or until the spices are toasted and fragrant.

Transfer contents to a blender. Add lemon juice and just enough oil to make a smooth purée. Season with salt and pepper. Set aside.

GLAZED EGGPLANT Cut eggplant slices into 3-inch pieces. Using a small knife, score the flesh on both sides of the eggplant pieces in a crosshatch pattern and season with salt and pepper.

Heat oil in a large skillet over high heat. Add eggplant pieces in a single layer, working in batches if necessary, and sear for 1 minute on each side, until golden brown. Reduce heat to medium, then add vinegar and honey. Simmer for 5 to 7 minutes, or until liquid is reduced to a glaze. Set aside.

M'HAMSA COUSCOUS

2 Tbsp extra-virgin olive oil

4 cloves garlic, chopped

4 cups chicken stock

2 cups M'hamsa couscous (see Note)

¼ tsp Harissa Spice Mix (see here)

Salt and white pepper, to taste

YOGURT SAUCE

1 seedless cucumber, peeled, seeded, and grated (1 cup)

1 tsp salt

2 cups plain Greek yogurt

4 cloves garlic, finely grated

¼ cup chopped mint

1 Tbsp grated lemon zest

White pepper, to taste

ASSEMBLY

Lamb (see here)

Fleur de sel, for sprinkling

A few pieces of lavash crackers (see Note)

Sprigs of mint

M'HAMSA COUSCOUS Heat oil in a medium saucepan over medium heat. Add garlic and sauté for 2 minutes, until translucent. Add stock and bring to a boil. Stir in couscous and spice mix and return to a boil. Remove from the heat, cover, and set aside for 7 minutes. Fluff with a fork. Season with salt and pepper.

YOGURT SAUCE Combine cucumber and salt in a bowl and set aside at room temperature for 10 minutes to extract moisture. Squeeze cucumber dry and transfer to a small bowl. Add the remaining ingredients and season to taste. Chill until ready to serve.

NOTE M'hamsa couscous is a type of whole wheat hand-rolled couscous that is mixed with olive oil and salt and left to dry in the sun. The result is a grain with a richer texture and depth of flavor. It can be purchased online. If needed, you can substitute with traditional couscous or, in a pinch, with instant couscous.

ASSEMBLY Preheat grill to medium-high heat.

Grill lamb on all sides for 5 minutes a side, until medium-rare and the internal temperature reaches 130°F. Transfer lamb to a cutting board and rest for 5 minutes. Slice.

Smear a spoonful of eggplant purée onto each plate. Add a spoonful of couscous to the side and top with three or four pieces of glazed eggplant. Arrange slices of lamb on top and sprinkle fleur de sel over the dish. Spoon some yogurt sauce beside the couscous and finish with a piece of lavash cracker and a sprig of mint.

NOTE Lavash crackers are thin sheet-pan crackers often enhanced with sesame seeds or Middle Eastern spices such as za'atar. They are available in most gourmet markets.

LINGUINE

Grated zest and juice
of 2 lemons

Pinch of Persian saffron
threads (see Note)

3½ cups "00" flour, plus
extra for dusting (1 lb)

1 cup semolina flour, plus
extra as needed (¼ lb)

½ tsp salt

Pinch of Persian saffron
powder (see Note)

5 medium eggs

Lemon-Saffron Linguine

SERVES 6 Pasta fiends will lust over Chef Daniel Boulud's note-perfect dish. Toothsome lemon-saffron linguine is served with savory clam sauce and topped with crisp breadcrumbs and rich bottarga. And guess what? It's every bit as delicious as you'd imagine it to be.

LINGUINE In a small saucepan, combine lemon juice and saffron threads and bring to a boil over high heat. Reduce heat to medium-low and simmer for 2 minutes. Remove from heat, cover, and set aside for 5 minutes.

In a food processor fitted with the paddle attachment, combine flours, salt, and saffron powder and process for 2 minutes. Add lemon zest and pulse. With the motor running, add the saffron-infused lemon juice, then add eggs, one at a time, and process until the dough comes together.

Transfer mixture to a floured work surface and knead by hand for 5 to 8 minutes, until smooth. (If making the dough well in advance of cooking, wrap in plastic wrap and refrigerate until needed.)

Divide dough into 4 equal pieces. Flatten each piece into a 3-inch square with a floured rolling pin. Roll the pieces of dough through a pasta machine until each is 12 × 5 inches and slightly translucent. Roll the sheets through a linguine-cutter attachment.

Line a baking sheet with a thin layer of semolina flour and place pasta on top. Sprinkle the pasta with more semolina to prevent sticking. Cover and refrigerate until ready to use.

NOTE Persian saffron is the best in terms of quality and the preferred saffron for this dish, but you can use any saffron available. Saffron threads are dried and ground to make saffron powder.

CLAMS

1 cup dry white wine

2 tsp chili flakes

4 cloves garlic, sliced

24 fresh littleneck clams, rinsed and scrubbed clean

ASSEMBLY

¼ cup extra-virgin olive oil

8 cloves garlic, finely chopped

1½ Tbsp chili flakes

1 fennel bulb, thinly shaved with a mandoline

3 cups arugula, packed

⅓ cup dry white wine

1 cup chicken stock

¼ cup (½ stick) butter

Linguine (see here)

Clams (see here)

1 cup coarse sourdough breadcrumbs

1 piece bottarga, very thinly sliced

CLAMS In a large saucepan over medium-high heat, combine wine, chili flakes, and garlic. Bring to a simmer, then reduce heat to medium-low and add clams. Cover and steam for 5 to 7 minutes, until shells open. Using a slotted spoon, transfer clams to a plate to cool. Cook the liquid for another 6 minutes, until reduced by half. Strain, then reserve in the pan.

Remove clams from the shells. Add clams to the pan and set aside until needed.

ASSEMBLY Heat oil in a large skillet over medium-low heat. Add garlic and chili flakes and cook for 2 minutes, until garlic is fragrant but not colored. Add fennel, increase heat to medium, and sauté for 4 minutes, until tender. Stir in arugula, then pour in wine and cook for 5 to 7 minutes, until the pan is nearly dry.

Pour in stock and simmer for 10 minutes, until reduced by half. Swirl in butter to emulsify.

Bring a stockpot of salted water to a boil. Add linguine and cook for 5 minutes, until al dente. Drain, then add to sauce and toss to combine. Add clams along with the liquid and toss for another 2 minutes, until well combined.

Transfer to warm pasta bowls and sprinkle with sourdough breadcrumbs and shaved bottarga. Serve immediately.

NOTE Bottarga is a pressed and cured fish roe that adds tremendous depth to a dish. Most chefs grate it like cheese and it adds a beautiful briny flavor. It can be found at gourmet markets.

CECCONI'S MIAMI BEACH

SERGIO SIGALA
executive chef

When it comes to great date spots in this city there are a few requirements: a picturesque garden, soulful food, perfectly dim, romantic lighting… and access to Miami's most stylish members-only club. Fulfilling all of the above, Cecconi's, a courtyard-heavy Italian stunner, has been fanning our pasta and celebrity-sighting fantasies since it opened back in 2010.

It is the kind of place that evokes lazy dinners on the Amalfi coast, with wooden communal tables, meticulously faded couches and chairs, and elegant details like olive trees strewn with twinkling lights. All this al fresco loveliness is tucked away behind the lobby at the Soho Beach House, an outpost of the members-only London club, which took over the refurbished Art Deco–era Sovereign Hotel. The restaurant is open to non-members, and its relaxed elegance vibe is well-suited to lunch-time client meetings over thin-crust pizzas, but it's also stylish enough for an evening spent

sipping Barolo under mason jar lanterns that hang from wooden beams.

Sergio Sigala, the former chef of Casa Tua, has been in the kitchen since Cecconi's first opened, and his baked gnocchi romana with gorgonzola has caused more than a few beauties to swoon with carb-induced delight. Here, attentive black-vested waiters prepare tuna tartare tableside and refresh baskets of sliced baguette and homemade grissini. Burrata and black truffles appear throughout the menu along with rich bowls of Maine lobster spaghetti (page 49) and, for those with Viking-sized appetites, the veal chop milanese. And I've saved the best for last: the entire restaurant is outdoors (there's a retractable roof in case it rains), allowing for easy dinners under the stars … making Miami feel very much like Italy, even if just for an evening.

SALMORIGLIO

6 black olives, pitted

2 Tbsp capers

1 Tbsp chopped Italian parsley

1 tsp chili flakes

1 tsp grated lemon zest

½ cup extra-virgin olive oil

BEEF TARTARE

10 oz USDA prime beef tenderloin, cut into ¼-inch cubes, covered and refrigerated until needed

¼ cup shaved Pecorino Romano

2 Tbsp finely chopped Italian parsley

1 Tbsp finely chopped celery

2 tsp Salmoriglio (see here)

Pinch of truffle salt

1 tsp extra-virgin olive oil

½ tsp truffle oil

Few drops of lemon juice

4 quail egg yolks

Crostini, to serve

Beef Tartare

SERVES 4 This elevated version of the classic delicacy is popular at Cecconi's for good reason. Hand-chopped beef is combined with the likes of *salmoriglio* (an Italian blend of olives, capers, parsley, chili flakes, and lemon zest), quail egg yolks, and truffle oil. Prime-grade beef is an essential starting point.

SALMORIGLIO In a food processor, combine all ingredients, except the oil, and pulse. With the motor running, gradually add oil until emulsified. (Leftover salmoriglio can be stored in an airtight container in the refrigerator for up to five days.)

BEEF TARTARE In a nonreactive bowl, combine beef, Pecorino Romano, parsley, celery, salmoriglio, and truffle salt. Using a fork or the back of a spoon, mash ingredients until evenly combined. Finish with olive oil, truffle oil, and lemon juice.

Divide beef tartare among four plates. Top each with a quail egg yolk, and serve with crostini.

1 (1½-lb) live lobster

2 Tbsp extra-virgin olive oil (divided)

2 cloves garlic (divided)

Pinch of dried pepperoncino (Calabrian chili flakes)

1 oz brandy

2 ripe tomatoes, cut into ½-inch cubes (divided)

10 oz dry spaghetti

Pinch of Persian saffron threads

Basil leaves, for garnish

Salt and black pepper

Extra-virgin olive oil, for drizzling

Spaghetti with Lobster

SERVES 2 TO 4 Here is an amazing lobster recipe that you can easily prepare at home. Chef Sigala maximizes flavor by making the sauce with, and cooking the spaghetti in, the lobster water. It's impressive how a few simple ingredients—garlic, pepperoncino, tomatoes, and brandy—can bring so much flavor to this crowd-pleasing dish. Sigala also uses designer pasta for this dish: the Dolce & Gabbana spaghetti produced by the brand Di Martino, which is available online and at specialty markets.

Bring a stockpot of water to a boil. Carefully lower lobster into the water and boil for 6 minutes. Remove lobster from water, reserving the stockpot of water, and set aside to cool.

Using your hands, remove lobster meat from the body and claws and set aside until needed. Reserve the shells and break the head into small pieces.

Heat 1 tablespoon oil in a saucepan over medium-high heat. Add a garlic clove and the pepperoncino and sauté for 1 minute, until fragrant. Add the broken lobster head and the shell from the body and cook for 2 to 3 minutes, until the shell turns bright red. Add brandy and cook for 1 minute, until evaporated. Stir in half the tomatoes and add 2 cups reserved lobster water, enough to nearly cover the mixture. Simmer for 15 minutes, until reduced by half, then strain using a fine-mesh strainer. Discard solids and set aside reduced sauce until needed.

Bring the stockpot of lobster water and a teaspoon of salt to a boil. Add spaghetti and cook for 7 minutes, until nearly al dente. Drain, reserving 2 cups of cooking liquid. Set pasta aside. Transfer cooking liquid to a saucepan and cook for another 10 minutes, until slightly thickened.

Heat the remaining tablespoon of oil in a large saucepan over medium-high heat. Smash the remaining garlic clove and add it to the pan, along with the remaining tomatoes, the lobster meat, the saffron, and the reduced sauce. Add spaghetti and cook for another 3 to 4 minutes. (If it's too dry, add a bit of the cooking liquid.)

Transfer spaghetti to a serving platter. Garnish with basil, season with salt and black pepper, and drizzle with olive oil.

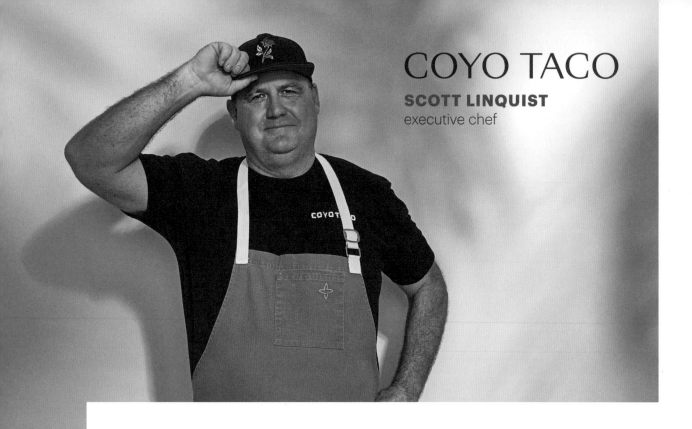

COYO TACO

SCOTT LINQUIST
executive chef

Miamians are obsessed with tacos and we can thank Coyo Taco for that. What started out as a hip Mexican taqueria with a backroom bar in Wynwood in 2015 has now expanded into a mini-empire with seven locations, including one in the Dominican Republic and another in Lisbon. Here in Miami, Chef Scott Linquist's tacos can be had at one of three locations—each with its own trademark clandestine bar brimming with tequila and mezcal cocktails and a live DJ—and at the bustling Time Out Market on Lincoln Road. Even Barack Obama is a fan, having stopped in when he passed through Miami.

But despite all the excitement (or because of it), the crowds keep returning for the things that made the original Coyo so popular: the fresh handmade tortillas prepared in the open kitchen (as many as 1,000 tortillas are prepared every day), a sustainably charged menu with humanely raised meats and locally sourced vegetables and seafood, and delicious, high-quality food.

Linquist cut his teeth as the national executive chef at New York's Dos Caminos restaurant group before branching out and developing Coyo with partners in Miami. His approach has always been simple: to respect the craft and tradition of Mexican cooking. "I spent over twenty years studying the history, culture, and cuisine of Mexico," he says. "The country's diverse landscape speaks to the culinary identity of each region, and I bring these profiles into my menus." At Coyo, he says, "I maintain the integrity of the dish, but I also throw in my signature 'mod-mex' twist." Tacos featuring slow-roasted pork shoulder with habanero pickled onions and crispy confit-style duck with serrano salsa (page 52) showcase Linquist's talents, and signal something uniquely modern and compelling on the taco scene.

FACING Duck Carnitas Tacos and Mexican Street Corn (*Esquites*)

DUCK

3 bay leaves, crumbled

1 stick canela (Mexican cinnamon), crumbled, or ¼ tsp ground cinnamon

1 cup salt

½ cup sugar

1 Tbsp chopped canned chipotles in adobo

2 tsp dried Mexican oregano

1 tsp black pepper

¼ tsp ground cloves

¼ tsp ground allspice

½ cup orange juice

3 lbs duck legs and thighs

DUCK CARNITAS

1 lb duck fat or lard

3 lbs Duck (see here)

1 onion, sliced

3 cloves garlic, crushed

6 black peppercorns

3 bay leaves

2 dried chipotle chiles

1 stick canela (Mexican cinnamon), or ¼ tsp ground cinnamon

Sprig of thyme

2 Tbsp salt

1 tsp dried Mexican oregano

½ cup orange juice

½ cup Coca-Cola

½ cup light Mexican beer (preferably Tecate)

½ cup condensed milk

Duck Carnitas Tacos

SERVES 4 Coyo Taco churns out some the best tacos in town, and fans flock to this top destination for the duck carnitas tacos. This signature favorite is loaded with duck, crispy red onions, tangy cheese, and fresh cilantro and doused with salsa for a lip-smacking meal. Pair them with an icy cold Modelo, and you have yourself a taste of comforting perfection.

DUCK In a large bowl, combine all ingredients except for the duck and mix well. Add duck and mix to evenly coat. Cover and refrigerate for 2 hours. Rinse duck under cold running water and pat dry with paper towels.

DUCK CARNITAS Preheat oven to 325°F.

Melt duck fat (or lard) in a roasting pan on the stovetop over medium heat. Add the duck, onion, garlic, peppercorns, bay leaves, chiles, canela (or cinnamon), thyme, salt, and oregano. Pour in juice, Coca-Cola, beer, and condensed milk. Bring to a simmer, then cover with aluminum foil. Roast in the oven for 2 hours, until meat is tender and falls from the bone. Set aside to cool.

SERRANO SALSA

8 tomatillos, peeled

1 small onion, quartered

4 cloves garlic

3 to 4 serrano chile peppers

¼ cup white wine vinegar

2 tsp dried Mexican oregano

2 Tbsp salt

Bunch of cilantro, roughly chopped

ASSEMBLY

Duck Carnitas (see here)

2 Tbsp duck fat or lard

Salt, to taste

12 6-inch corn tortillas

Serrano Salsa (see here)

1 red onion, finely chopped

1 cup grated cotija cheese or *queso añejo*

1 cup chopped cilantro

Tortilla chips, to serve (optional)

Guacamole, to serve (optional)

SERRANO SALSA Place all ingredients except the cilantro in a large saucepan and cover with water. Bring to a simmer over medium-high heat and cook for 8 to 10 minutes, until ingredients are cooked through. Remove from heat and set aside to cool.

Using a slotted spoon, transfer solid ingredients to a blender. Add cilantro and purée until smooth. Cover and set aside.

NOTE Duck fat and lard can be purchased at gourmet markets, butcher shops, and specialty meat retailers.

ASSEMBLY Using tongs, transfer duck to a baking rack to drain. Separate duck meat and skin from the bones and roughly chop. Discard bones. Cover duck carnitas and set aside.

Melt duck fat (or lard) in a large skillet over medium-high heat. Add duck carnitas and sauté for 8 minutes, until crispy and brown. Season with salt. Keep warm.

Heat a large dry skillet over medium heat. Add 2 tortillas and heat for 2 minutes on each side, until warm. Wrap in aluminum foil. Repeat with remaining tortillas.

Place three tortillas on each plate and spoon 2 tablespoons of duck carnitas onto each one. Drizzle with salsa and top with red onions, cheese, and cilantro. Serve immediately with plenty of extra salsa and chips and guacamole, if desired.

CHIPOTLE AIOLI

1 cup mayonnaise

2 Tbsp honey

1 Tbsp chopped canned chipotles in adobo

1 Tbsp lime juice

CORN

2 Tbsp vegetable oil

4 ears sweet corn

2 Tbsp lime juice

½ tsp salt

ASSEMBLY

4 cups Corn (see here)

½ cup Chipotle Aioli (see here)

½ cup grated cotija cheese or *queso añejo*

2 Tbsp chopped cilantro

Pinch of chili powder (optional)

4 lime wedges

Mexican Street Corn (Esquites)

SERVES 4 This dish is an off-the-cob version of *elote,* the popular grilled corn Mexican street food dish. Slathered with chipotle-spiked mayo and lime, this corn salad makes for a spicy satisfying snack or colorful side dish for a Mexican meal.

CHIPOTLE AIOLI Purée all ingredients in a blender until smooth. Set aside.

CORN Heat oil in a large skillet over high heat. Carefully add corn (so not to splash the hot oil) and gently cook for 8 minutes, until lightly browned on all sides. Season with lime juice and salt. Transfer to a cutting board and set aside to cool slightly, then stand each ear of corn straight up and use a knife to gently shave kernels off.

ASSEMBLY Divide corn into four small bowls, top each with 2 tablespoons chipotle aioli, 2 tablespoons cheese, and cilantro, and dust with chili powder, if using. Serve with lime wedges.

CRUST

KLIME KOVACESKI
executive chef and co-owner

ANITA KOVACESKI
co-owner

Chef Klime Kovaceski spent most of his career in fine dining, having steered the kitchen at Miami Beach's Crystal Café for years and then working as a consultant for upscale restaurants. In 2015, the Macedonia-born chef decided to launch a casual pizza joint on the Miami River called Crust, with the goal of doing mostly takeout and delivery service. His Aussie wife, Anita, gave up her advertising job to run the front of house and the two embarked on running what they thought would be a humble neighborhood spot.

"Crust was designed to be 80% take out and delivery and 20% a dine-in restaurant," Klime explains. "But it turned out to be the other way around!" The warm, welcoming spot quickly became one of the most popular restaurants in the city, with rave reviews on social media sites like TripAdvisor and Yelp and a flattering profile by *The Wall Street Journal* highlighting the restaurant's success in an industry where many others fail.

The power couple's attention to detail is legendary, from personally greeting every table to answering social media queries to Klime working the line in the kitchen and training each employee. They are committed to making every guest's dining experience special, and that dedication has paid off. Diners flock to the restaurant for generously portioned Italian classics served with the kind of easy hospitality guided by the owners' personal compass.

"Crust is a stable business, with a nice mixture of regulars, locals, and visitors," says Klime. "We're grateful that the restaurant is pretty busy year-round."

FACING Shrimp Cakes

SAUTÉED MUSHROOMS

3 Tbsp butter

1 lb white button mushrooms, sliced

2 Tbsp mixed chopped herbs, such as basil, oregano, and/or thyme

½ Tbsp salt

½ Tbsp black pepper

TOMATO COULIS

¼ cup canola-olive oil blend

½ onion, chopped (½ cup)

¼ cup chopped garlic

1 bay leaf

4 cups canned whole tomatoes

2 Tbsp sugar

2 Tbsp salt

1 Tbsp black pepper

1 Tbsp chopped basil

½ cup (1 stick) butter, cubed

GARLIC AIOLI

2 egg yolks

2 cloves garlic

1 tsp Dijon mustard

1 tsp lemon juice

½ cup vegetable blend oil or canola oil

½ cup olive oil

½ cup chopped fresh spinach

½ cup chopped fresh basil

Salt and black pepper, to taste

SHRIMP CAKES

2 lbs shrimp, peeled, deveined, and chopped

2 leeks, white and light green parts only, chopped

2 Roma tomatoes, chopped

3 organic eggs

3 Tbsp chopped basil

2 cups panko breadcrumbs, plus extra if needed (divided)

¼ cup canola oil

Salt and black pepper, to taste

Basil oil, to serve

Basil sprigs, for garnish

Shrimp Cakes

MAKES 12 A riff on the classic crab cake, this dish is an easy go-to when you're looking for an elevated quick-fix or a hearty brunch course.

SAUTÉED MUSHROOMS Melt butter in a saucepan over medium heat. Add mushrooms and herbs and sauté for 6 to 8 minutes, or until mushrooms are tender. Add salt and pepper and cook for another 5 minutes. Remove from heat, cover, and set aside.

TOMATO COULIS Heat oil in a large saucepan over low heat. Add onion, garlic, and bay leaf and sauté for 7 minutes, until onions are translucent. Add tomatoes, sugar, salt, pepper, and basil and cook for 15 minutes, stirring occasionally, or until all the excess moisture has evaporated. Remove bay leaf.

Transfer mixture to blender, working batches if necessary, and purée until smooth. Whisk in butter and set aside.

GARLIC AIOLI In a food processor, blend together egg yolks, garlic, Dijon mustard, and lemon juice. Drizzle the oils in slowly until the mixture reaches a mayo-like consistency. Add spinach and basil and blend until smooth. Season with salt and pepper. Set aside.

SHRIMP CAKES In a large mixing bowl, combine shrimp, leeks, tomatoes, eggs, and basil. Stir in 1½ cups panko breadcrumbs and set aside for 5 minutes to thicken up enough to hold together. If needed, add more breadcrumbs.

Divide mixture into 12 equal portions. Shape each into a 3-inch patty, about 1 inch thick. Put the remaining ½ cup panko breadcrumbs in a shallow bowl. Add cakes and coat all over.

Heat oil in a skillet over medium-high heat. Add shrimp cakes, working in batches if necessary, and pan-fry for 5 minutes on each side, until golden brown and cooked through.

ASSEMBLY Spread 3 tablespoons of tomato coulis onto the center of each plate. Spoon a tablespoon of garlic aioli onto the middle of the tomato coulis. Add mushrooms, then place two shrimp cakes on top. Season with salt and pepper, drizzle basil oil around the plate, garnish with basil sprigs, and serve immediately.

SEAFOOD

- 1 Tbsp canola-olive oil blend
- 1 clove garlic, chopped
- 2 Tbsp chopped shallots
- 2 Tbsp chopped leeks
- ½ cup clam juice
- ½ cup chicken stock
- ¼ cup canned crushed tomatoes
- Pinch of saffron
- ¼ lb shrimp, peeled and deveined
- ¼ lb mussels, rinsed and scrubbed clean
- ¼ lb scallops
- ¼ cup sliced squid
- ¼ cup chopped clams
- 1 tsp chopped basil
- 1 Tbsp butter
- Salt and black pepper, to taste

RISOTTO

- 1 cup arborio rice
- 2 cups warm chicken stock, plus extra if needed
- 1 tsp chopped basil
- Seafood (see here)

Seafood Risotto

SERVES 2 This isn't a traditional risotto but it's just as tasty, with a medley of seafood that works well with the richness of the creamy rice. Complete the meal with a salad, bread, and crisp white wine.

SEAFOOD Heat oil in a saucepan over medium-high heat. Add garlic, shallots, and leeks and sauté for 1 minute. Add clam juice, chicken stock, tomatoes, and saffron. Bring to a simmer and cook for 2 to 3 minutes, until reduced by a quarter.

Add shrimp, mussels, scallops, squid, clams, and basil and cook for 3 minutes, until mussel shells open up. Stir in butter and season with salt and pepper. Remove from heat and discard any unopened shells. Set aside.

RISOTTO In a large skillet, combine rice, stock, and basil over medium heat. Simmer for 10 to 12 minutes, stirring occasionally, until rice is al dente. If needed, add more stock. Add seafood to the rice and cook for another 3 minutes.

Serve in shallow bowls, arranging the pieces of seafood on top of the rice.

EDGE STEAK & BAR

AARON BROOKS
executive chef

HECTOR LLOMPART
pastry chef

Aaron Brooks will be the first to tell you that he knew very little about Miami's Latin cuisine when he was tapped to run the modern steakhouse at downtown's glitzy Four Seasons Hotel Miami in 2011. But the gregarious Aussie quickly set about getting to know the culinary scene here, picking up flavor profiles and techniques from fellow chefs and incorporating them into his ever-changing non-traditional steakhouse menu. Now Brooks has become a fixture of the local culinary community, regularly hosting chef showdowns, cook-offs, and poolside barbecues.

Also known as Miami's "Lambassador" by True Aussie Beef & Lamb, Brooks is particularly drawn to the Latin and Caribbean flavors that make Miami so dynamic, and their versatility with grilled meats. It's why he shares his lamb anticuchos recipe with us (page 62). "It was a fun twist to meld new flavors with lamb, a protein that I grew up with." He is also well known for his in-house charcuterie, plus his ceviches and crudos.

And don't be fooled by EDGE Steak & Bar's steakhouse categorization—the veggie dishes are as exciting as the meats, with Chef Brooks sending out seasonal dishes such as endive salad with Point Reyes blue cheese and roasted radishes with a lavender-honey vinaigrette.

Likewise, EDGE's pastry chef Hector Llompart's desserts are driven by tropical flavors that are embedded in his Puerto Rican roots and showcased throughout the decadent dessert menu. His creations deftly balance sweetness with acidity and brightness, like in the sour cream panna cotta with grapefruit ginger ice cream or in the complex chocolate namelaka with coconut crumble (page 63)—every one is a fitting coda to the indulgent experience at EDGE.

FACING Aussie Lamb Anticuchos with Baby Potatoes and Chile Sauce

AJI PANCA MARINADE

7 Tbsp white vinegar

5 Tbsp aji panca paste

¼ cup soy sauce

3 Tbsp canola-olive oil blend

1½ Tbsp garlic powder

1 Tbsp dried oregano

2 tsp ground cumin

LAMB ANTICUCHOS WITH BABY POTATOES

2 lbs Aussie grass-fed lamb loins, cut into 1-inch chunks

1 cup Aji Panca Marinade (see here)

24 baby marble potatoes, unpeeled

1 Tbsp salt

AJI AMARILLO SAUCE

½ cup canola-olive oil blend

1 white onion, chopped

3 cloves garlic, chopped

¾ cup aji amarillo paste

1 Tbsp chopped cilantro

1 Tbsp chopped scallions

Juice of 4 limes

ASSEMBLY

Salt, to taste

Leafy or quinoa salad, to serve (optional)

Limes halves, to serve

Aussie Lamb Anticuchos with Baby Potatoes and Chile Sauce

SERVES 4 Chef Brooks recommends marinating the lamb overnight but notes that these tasty anticuchos can be prepared on the same day if you're pressed for time. Plus, any leftover aji panca marinade can add a flavorful punch to other grilled meats.

AJI PANCA MARINADE Using an immersion blender, combine all ingredients in a small bowl. (Leftover marinade can be stored in the refrigerator for up to seven days.)

LAMB ANTICUCHOS WITH BABY POTATOES In a large bowl, combine lamb loin and marinade and refrigerate at least 1 hour or overnight.

Bring a saucepan of water to a boil. Add potatoes and salt and simmer for 25 minutes, until softened. Drain, then refrigerate along with the lamb.

AJI AMARILLO SAUCE Heat oil in a skillet over medium heat. Add onion and garlic and sauté for 5 to 7 minutes, until softened. Add remaining ingredients and cook for another 5 minutes. Transfer mixture to a blender and blend until smooth. Set aside to cool.

ASSEMBLY Preheat grill to high heat.

Skewer lamb and potatoes evenly among 12 metal skewers. Season with salt and grill for 3 to 4 minutes on each side, until cooked through. Transfer to a platter.

Drizzle aji amarillo sauce and leftover aji panca marinade over the skewers. Serve immediately with salad, if using, and limes.

NOTE Aji panca paste is derived from a type of chile pepper that is commonly grown in Peru and frequently used in Peruvian cuisine. Aji amarillo paste is made from Peruvian peppers that are bright orange-yellow and pack some punch. Both pastes can be found at local gourmet markets or online.

ORELYS NAMELAKA

1 sheet gold-strength gelatin (see Note)

½ cup whole milk

1 tsp glucose (see Note)

1½ cups Valrhona Blond Orelys 35% chocolate, chopped

¾ cup whipping cream

COCONUT CRUMBLE

1¼ cups all-purpose flour

¾ cup shredded coconut

⅔ cup almond flour

½ cup (1 stick) butter

½ cup packed brown sugar

PASSIONFRUIT GRANITE

⅔ cup sugar

1 cup passionfruit purée

ASSEMBLY

1 banana, sliced

Orelys Chocolate Namelaka with Coconut Crumble, Passionfruit Granite, and Banana Slices

SERVES 4 This impressive dessert by pastry chef Hector Llompart tastes as good as it looks. *Namelaka*, the Japanese term for creamy/smooth, is a cross between a ganache and a *crème pâtissière*. Here, it is enhanced with Valrhona chocolate and accented with passionfruit granite and a satisfying coconut crumble.

ORELYS NAMELAKA Place gelatin in a small bowl of ice water for 5 to 10 minutes, until softened.

In a small saucepan, combine milk and glucose and simmer over low heat for 4 minutes, until well combined. Add gelatin and stir.

Place chocolate in a stainless steel or glass bowl. Pour in milk mixture and use a whisk to blend until smooth. Stir in cream.

Pour mixture into four serving vessels and refrigerate overnight to set.

NOTE Sheet gelatin is graded by different strengths of bloom: bronze, silver, gold, and platinum. The different varieties can be found at specialty supermarkets or online.

Glucose is a syrup with less sweetness than table sugar. Professional pastry chefs use it to lend texture to desserts.

COCONUT CRUMBLE Preheat oven to 350°F. Line a baking sheet with parchment paper.

In a stand mixer fitted with a paddle attachment, combine all ingredients and mix on slow speed.

Spread evenly over the prepared baking sheet and cook for 12 minutes, until golden brown. Remove from oven and set aside to cool to room temperature. Store leftover crumble in an airtight container.

PASSIONFRUIT GRANITE In a small saucepan, combine sugar and 1 cup water and bring to a boil. Remove from heat, then set aside to cool.

Whisk in passionfruit purée. Pour mixture into a shallow container and place in freezer.

Using a fork, scrape all through the mixture every 30 minutes for about 2 hours, until it is crumbly and has a firm crystal-like consistency. Keep frozen until ready to serve.

ASSEMBLY Remove namelaka servings from refrigerator. Sprinkle coconut crumble on top, add banana slices, and then top each with a spoonful of passionfruit granite. Serve immediately.

EMBER

BRAD KILGORE
owner and executive chef

Brad Kilgore is a chef known for meticulously plated, almost molecular-gastronomy-style cooking at Alter, his first restaurant in Wynwood. So it came as a surprise to the city's dining community when he opened Ember, a wood-fired American bistro with a focus on big, meaty mains. The fourth restaurant in his burgeoning Kilgore Culinary Group empire, this cushy spot is also a stylistic departure from the polished concrete urbanism of Alter, outfitted as it is in white oak and camel-colored leather. And the menu at Ember is hearty and belly-filling: think mashed potatoes, crispy fried oysters, cornbread, and beef stroganoff.

"Ember is an homage to the restaurant where I learned to cook and the dishes I love to eat on my days off," says Kansas-born Kilgore, who is no stranger to barbecue and its trappings. "I love to cook with fire, slow-smoke things, and work with the element of char by taking unconventional dishes and ingredients to the grill. We're doing a grilled lasagna, for example, and cooking a terrine over the embers and finishing it with a demi-glace."

It's the kind of place we return to again and again for its unapologetic gluttony. We're talking fried chicken with caviar butter and the Rice Krispie treats that are made in-house. "I want Ember to be known as a place for good food, whether in the neighborhood or Miami in general."

FACING Cornbread with Short Rib Ragout and Rum Cake Mai Tai

BONE MARROW

3 Tbsp salt

2 bay leaves

5 marrow bones

SHORT RIBS

¼ cup grapeseed oil

1 lb boneless Black Angus short ribs

1 head garlic, top sliced off

½ large red onion, chopped

1 (2-inch) piece ginger, peeled and sliced (¼ cup)

2 scallions, chopped

2 Tbsp red wine vinegar

1 cup red wine

6 cups sliced shiitake mushrooms

½ cup ABC sweet soy sauce (also known as Indonesian sweet soy sauce)

¼ cup brewed coffee

Chicken stock, if needed

BONE-MARROW BUTTER

Bone Marrow (see here)

2 cups (4 sticks) + 1 Tbsp butter, softened (divided)

1 Tbsp finely chopped shallots

1 Tbsp finely chopped Meyer lemon, with skin

1 Tbsp chopped chives

1 Tbsp chopped Italian parsley

1 tsp salt

1 tsp black pepper

Cornbread with Short Rib Ragout

SERVES 4 Humble and hearty cornbread gets the Brad Kilgore treatment: here, it's smothered in bone-marrow butter and topped with luscious slow-cooked short ribs bathed in a red wine jus. The fresh and vibrant herb salad with its beautiful shallot vinaigrette cuts through the richness and offsets all that indulgence. Make sure to start a day in advance, to soak the marrow bones.

BONE MARROW In a large bowl, combine salt, bay leaves, and 5 cups cold water. Add marrow bones and soak for 24 hours.

SHORT RIBS Preheat oven to 290°F.

Heat oil in a skillet over high heat. Add short ribs and brown for 3 minutes on each side. Transfer short ribs to a deep baking dish and set aside.

Place garlic, cut-side down, in the same skillet and add onion, ginger, and scallions to the pan. Cook for 3 minutes, until garlic is slightly charred. Add vinegar, then pour in wine and cook for 5 to 7 minutes, until the liquid is reduced by a third. Add mushrooms, soy sauce, and coffee and bring to a simmer. Pour mixture over short ribs in baking dish. If necessary, top up with enough stock to cover. Cook for 3 hours, until ribs are tender and cooked through. Set aside to cool to room temperature.

BONE-MARROW BUTTER Preheat oven to 325°F.

Transfer soaked marrow bones to a roasting pan and roast for 15 minutes. Set aside to cool. Carefully remove marrow from bones, avoiding bone fragments. Set aside.

Melt 1 tablespoon butter in a skillet over medium heat. Add shallots and sauté for 4 minutes, until softened. Remove from heat.

In a large bowl, combine bone marrow, the 2 cups butter, and the remaining ingredients and mix until well combined and the butter has flecks of marrow. Cover and set aside.

RED WINE JUS Heat oil in a large saucepan over medium heat. Add shallots and sauté for 10 minutes, until golden and caramelized. Add garlic, fennel seeds, and peppercorns and sauté for 2 minutes.

Pour in Port and wine, then add bay leaves and rosemary. Simmer for 10 minutes, or until reduced by half.

RED WINE JUS

¼ cup extra-virgin olive oil

2 shallots, finely chopped

20 cloves garlic, sliced using a mandoline (¾ cup)

3 Tbsp fennel seeds

2 Tbsp black peppercorns

1¾ cups Port wine

1½ cups red wine

3 bay leaves

2 sprigs rosemary

1½ cups demi-glace (see Note)

2 Tbsp butter

CORNBREAD

4 cups milk

1 Tbsp white vinegar

2 cups all-purpose flour

1½ cups cornmeal

1½ cups sugar

1 tsp baking soda

1 tsp salt

4 eggs

2 Tbsp butter

SHALLOT VINAIGRETTE

1 cup grapeseed oil (divided)

3 shallots, chopped (1 cup)

3 cloves garlic, sliced

Pinch of salt

Pinch of black pepper

Pinch of fennel seeds

½ cup sherry vinegar

½ cup red wine vinegar

1 Tbsp honey

HERB SALAD

¼ cup pea shoots

¼ cup chopped chives

¼ cup frisée

¼ cup chopped Italian parsley

¼ cup chervil

½ cup Shallot Vinaigrette (see here)

Salt, to taste

Pickled onions, for garnish (optional)

Pour in demi-glace and cook for another 8 minutes, until reduced by half. Strain and discard solids. Transfer sauce to a new pan and bring to a boil, then remove from the heat and whisk in butter. Set aside.

CORNBREAD Preheat oven to 350°F.

In a large bowl, combine milk and vinegar and set aside for 5 to 10 minutes, until mixture turns lumpy.

In a separate bowl, combine flour, cornmeal, sugar, baking soda, and salt. Whisk eggs into the soured milk. Stir wet mixture into dry ingredients and set aside.

Melt butter in a large cast-iron skillet over low heat. Pour in batter, then place skillet into oven and bake for 45 minutes, until golden brown on top.

NOTE *Demi-glace,* made from veal stock, is a gourmet item that can be found at fine food stores or online. Alternatively, use a premium beef base (located in the soup and stock aisle of supermarkets) and thicken with a little cornstarch.

SHALLOT VINAIGRETTE Heat ½ cup oil in a skillet over high heat, until nearly smoking. Add shallots and sauté for 20 seconds, until edges begin to color. Add garlic and cook for another 2 to 3 minutes, until the edges brown. Turn off heat, then stir in salt, pepper, and fennel seeds.

Transfer mixture to a blender and blend until smooth. Add vinegars and honey, then strain through a fine-mesh sieve, discarding solids. Set aside.

HERB SALAD In a bowl, combine all ingredients and toss gently.

ASSEMBLY Remove short ribs from the braising liquid and shred by hand. Combine short ribs and 1 cup red wine jus and bring to a boil. Reduce heat to medium-low and simmer for 10 minutes, adding a little more red wine jus if needed but keeping the ragout thick.

Serve the cornbread in the skillet, family-style, and top each serving with 3 to 4 tablespoons of short rib ragout. Serve with herb salad and bone-marrow butter on the side. Garnish with pickled onions, if using.

¼ cup Caribbean rum

2 Tbsp orgeat syrup or
  amaretto (see Note)

Juice of ½ lemon

1 Tbsp maple syrup

1 egg yolk

Candied pecans,
  for garnish

Rum Cake Mai Tai

SERVES 1 The classic Polynesian cocktail gets dessert treatment with the addition of maple syrup and a frothy egg yolk for a creamy finish. The candied pecan garnish suggests Thanksgiving in a glass. Candied pecans are available at gourmet and specialty grocers.

Shake together all liquid ingredients and serve over a large ice cube. Garnish with candied pecans.

NOTE Orgeat syrup is a nutty, floral sweetener often used in tropical cocktails and it can be found online. In a pinch, you can substitute it with amaretto.

FINKA
TABLE & TAP

EILEEN ANDRADE
owner and executive chef

Chef Eileen Andrade grew up in the restaurant business. Her grandparents started Islas Canarias, the shrine of Cuban comfort food, and she could have easily slipped into a position in her family's thriving dining empire. Instead, she decided to strike out on her own. Seeing a dearth of creative gastropubs in western Miami-Dade serving the kind of food she liked—a mélange of Korean, Cuban, and Peruvian influences—she created Finka.

The place has been packed since day one, with suburbanites hungering for Andrade's thoughtfully-tweaked comfort food. You'll find chicken drumsticks cloaked in the Korean fermented chili paste *gochujang*, tostones topped with tender strands of *ropa vieja* and Peruvian pico de gallo, and the Cuban bibimbap bowl, featuring *vaca frita* (crispy beef), black beans, *maduros* (fried sweet plantains), kimchi, and a fried egg on a bed of rice.

So much about Andrade's cool Westchester spot feels like a beacon in a storm—everything we love about dining in Miami right now all under a single roof. Some might be tempted to call it indecisive, and if all of it wasn't so mind-bendingly delicious, we might do the same. Instead, we're going to call Andrade a phenomenon. She's a chef who has as much range as she does a sense of humor, and an uncanny understanding of exactly what we want to eat and how we want to eat it. In a word: *dale*.

- 4 lbs oxtail, fat trimmed
- Salt and black pepper
- 3 Tbsp olive oil
- 6 cloves garlic, finely chopped
- 1 Spanish onion, chopped
- 1 green bell pepper, seeded, deveined, and finely chopped
- 1 red bell pepper, seeded, deveined, and finely chopped
- 1 carrot, chopped
- 2 Tbsp tomato paste
- 2 cups beef stock
- 1 cup red wine
- ½ tsp allspice
- ½ tsp ground cumin
- 4 bay leaves
- Crusty bread, to serve

Cuban-Style Oxtail Stew

SERVES 4 When the temperature drops, you'll find fortification and nourishment in comforting stews—and this recipe is no exception. Fork-tender oxtail and chunky vegetables are cooked low and slow in a savory tomato-based stock. All that's required is some crusty bread to mop up the juices.

Season all sides of oxtail with salt and pepper.

Heat oil in a large Dutch oven over high heat. Working in batches if needed, add oxtail and sear each piece for 8 minutes, turning occasionally, until browned on all sides. Transfer oxtail to a plate.

In the same pot, sauté garlic, onion, peppers and carrots for 5 to 7 minutes, until tender. Return oxtail to pot, then add tomato paste, stock, and wine. Bring to a boil, then reduce heat to medium-low. Add allspice, cumin, and bay leaves and simmer for 2½ to 3 hours, until oxtail is fork tender. Season with salt and pepper to taste and serve with crusty bread.

MARINADE

5 cloves garlic, finely chopped

3 Tbsp brown sugar

½ tsp grated ginger

¼ tsp black pepper

4½ Tbsp soy sauce

3 Tbsp concentrated pear juice (see Note)

2 Tbsp mirin

1½ tsp sesame oil

CHICKEN

2 lbs bone-in chicken thighs

Marinade (see here)

5 to 6 oz Korean glass noodles (sweet potato starch noodles)

Sesame oil, for searing

5 dried red chiles (divided)

2 potatoes, peeled and cut into 1-inch cubes

1 large Spanish onion, coarsely chopped

1 carrot, chopped

5 button mushrooms, thinly sliced

2 scallions, roughly chopped

Korean Braised Chicken with Glass Noodles

SERVES 2 TO 3 This popular Korean dish, also known as *Andong jjimdak,* originates in the city of Andong, Korea. All at once savory, sweet, and spicy, it sees spicy braised chicken cooked together with Korean glass noodles for a dish that explodes with flavor.

MARINADE Combine all ingredients in a small bowl and mix well.

NOTE Korean cooking often calls for pear juice for marinating and tenderizing meat. It can be found in most Asian markets.

CHICKEN In a large bowl, combine chicken and marinade, turning to coat, and refrigerate for 1 hour.

Soak glass noodles in water for 20 minutes, until softened.

Coat a large skillet with sesame oil and bring to high heat. Add 3 chiles and sauté for 5 to 7 minutes, until the chiles darken. Discard chiles.

Add chicken to the skillet, reserving marinade, and sear for 4 minutes on each side, until browned. Transfer chicken to a plate.

In a large saucepan over high heat, combine the reserved marinade and 4 cups of water. Bring to a boil, then add chicken, reduce heat to medium, and simmer for 10 to 15 minutes, until chicken is almost fully cooked. Add the remaining 2 chiles and the potatoes, onion, and carrot and simmer for 5 to 8 minutes, until vegetables are softened. Add noodles, mushrooms, and scallions and simmer for another 6 to 8 minutes, until noodles are cooked. Remove the 2 chiles, if desired, and serve immediately.

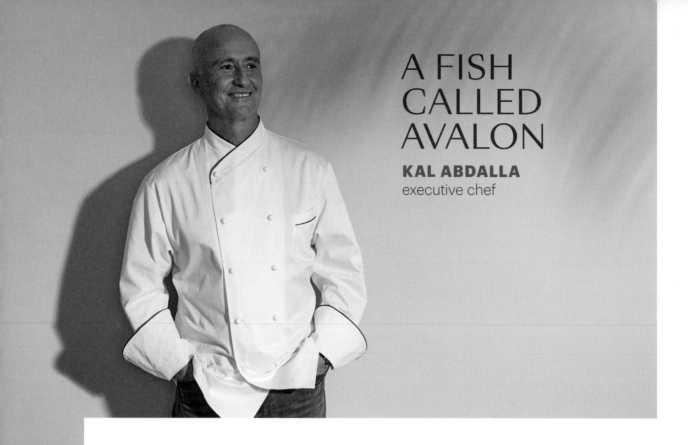

A FISH CALLED AVALON

KAL ABDALLA
executive chef

Thirty years ago, A Fish Called Avalon set the bar for upscale seafood restaurants on South Beach: namely, great service, a top-notch chef, and an enduring menu that would stand the test of time on a bustling stretch of Ocean Drive. A celebrated Art Deco landmark, the restaurant has served as a backdrop for many films and photo shoots throughout the years, including *Scarface* and *Miami Vice*. The iconic 1955 Oldsmobile convertible parked in front of the restaurant is one of the most photographed cars in America.

The restaurant has thrived the past decade under the direction of Executive Chef Kal Abdalla. A veteran of The Forge and a native of the Syrian island of Arwad, Abdalla masterfully adds layers of flavor and texture to modern American dishes and infuses his recipes with an appreciation of the Mediterranean's bountiful fish, seafood, and fruits and vegetables. Dishes such as the macadamia-crusted snapper and

the sake-tarragon glazed lobster tails keep locals and tourists coming back despite the rampant competition in South Beach. Seafood is served with carefully considered accompaniments: the orzo seafood paella (page 76) is infused with a saffron-tinged tomato broth while the bang bang shrimp are dressed with a turmeric-curry spice blend.

In a city surrounded by water we have very few places that focus solely on the treasures of the sea, and that's what distinguishes Avalon from its South Beach counterparts.

FACING Orzo Seafood Paella

- 1 cup orzo
- 2 Tbsp extra-virgin olive oil
- 3 cloves garlic, chopped
- 2 Tbsp chopped shallots
- 2 Tbsp chopped basil
- ½ cup sliced calamari
- 6 large mussels, rinsed and scrubbed clean
- 4 large shrimp, cleaned and deveined
- 2 jumbo scallops
- Salt and black pepper
- 1 tomato, cut into wedges
- ¼ small carrot, finely chopped
- 2 cups baby spinach
- Pinch of saffron
- 1 cup clam juice
- ½ cup Chardonnay
- Juice of 1 lemon
- 1 (1 lb) Maine lobster, lightly steamed and split in half
- Baby beet greens, for garnish

Orzo Seafood Paella

SERVES 2 This playful rendition of traditional Spanish paella subs out the rice for orzo pasta, which is quicker to cook and creates a perfect backdrop to saffron-tinged broth and seafood.

Preheat oven to 425°F.

Cook orzo until al dente, according to package directions. Set aside.

Heat oil in a large skillet over medium heat. Add garlic, shallots, and basil and sauté briefly, then add calamari, mussels, shrimp, and scallops. Sauté for 1 minute, then season with salt and pepper. Add the remaining ingredients, except for the lobster, beet greens, and orzo and stir for 1 minute.

Place the split lobster in a paella pan or an ovenproof skillet, then top with the seafood mixture and bake for 8 minutes. Serve over orzo and garnish with baby beet greens.

SOUFFLÉ

1½ cups egg whites

2 cups confectioners' sugar

Juice of 2 lemons

2 tsp grated lemon zest

CREPES

1¾ cups all-purpose flour

¼ cup vegetable oil

2 cups whole milk

2 eggs

Cooking spray

Raspberries, for garnish

Confectioners' sugar, for dusting

Guiltless Lemon Soufflé Crepes

SERVES 4 For this dessert, Chef Kal Abdalla combines a yolk-free soufflé (hence guiltless) with a crepe. The result is a wonderfully refreshing, yet not too indulgent, coda to a seafood feast and one of Avalon's most popular desserts.

SOUFFLÉ Using an electric mixer, whip egg whites on high speed until creamy and semi-stiff. Reduce speed to medium-high and gradually add sugar. Reduce speed to low, then add lemon juice and lemon zest. Set aside.

CREPES Preheat oven to 425°F.

In a bowl, combine flour, oil, milk, and eggs and beat until smooth.

Lightly coat a skillet with cooking spray and heat over medium-high heat. Pour in 2 tablespoons of batter and swirl so a thin layer coats the pan. Cook for 30 seconds, until the crepe separates from the pan. Flip and cook for another 30 seconds.

Add 1 cup soufflé mixture to the center of the crepe, fold crepe over, and transfer to a baking dish. Repeat with the remaining batter, layering the crepes if needed, then bake for 5 minutes, or until light golden brown.

Transfer crepes to serving plates, then garnish with raspberries and dust with confectioners' sugar.

FOOQ'S

DAVID FOULQUIER
owner

In 2015, when young restaurateur David Foulquier opened this homey downtown spot inspired by his Persian and French background, not many folks knew what to make of it. The menu featured a global bouquet of Persian, French, American, and Italian flavors. The tiny space was warmed up with upholstered benches, colorful cushions, antlers, cookbooks, and Moroccan-style tables. Was it a gastropub for artsy types? An eclectic post-theater spot for Arsht Center patrons? A late-night pasta hang for cocktail lovers from the neighboring bar The Corner? Yes, yes, and yes.

As its owner has matured and gone on to open Michelin star–earning establishments in New York and elsewhere, so too has Fooq's settled into a relaxed zone of creating and serving interesting comfort food. The menu's Persian dishes are no doubt what set it apart from practically any restaurant in Miami—from an ever-changing daily *khoresh,* or stew, to

the "jeweled" rice festooned with dried fruits and saffron that is a marvel of crunch and spice. The Persian influence shows up again in a "sundae" made with saffron, rosewater, and pistachio gelato (page 81) and roasted pistachios and other toppings. But there's also the Bucatini Amatriciana that's been a hit since day one and the fantastic burger with its towering double patty and special sauce.

It's what Foulquier has called "feel good food" and that's what has made this quirky little spot on the outskirts of downtown a destination on its own.

FACING Persian Carrot and Sour Cherry Stew
(*Khoresh Havij Ba Aloo*)

HAVIJ SPICE MIX

¼ cup garam masala

¼ cup brown sugar

1 Tbsp ground turmeric

1 tsp chili flakes

STEW

2 Tbsp canola oil

2 large onions, thinly sliced

Salt

15 carrots (3 lbs), cut into 2- x ¼-inch batons

3 cloves garlic, thinly sliced

¼ cup Havij Spice Mix (see here)

1½ cups dried sour cherries

Basmati rice, to serve

Salad greens, to serve

Persian Carrot and Sour Cherry Stew (Khoresh Havij Ba Aloo)

SERVES 6 TO 8 A lighter take on Persian stew (khoresh), this vegan-friendly version foregoes traditional beef or lamb and incorporates dried cherries for a tart finish. The result is a fantastic vegetable dish that makes for a satisfying main when served with rice and salad. The leftover havij spice mix can be used as a great seasoning for most stewed vegetable dishes.

HAVIJ SPICE MIX Combine all ingredients in a spice grinder and pulse to mix. Store in an airtight container.

STEW Heat oil in a saucepan over medium-high heat. Add onions and a pinch of salt and sauté for 20 minutes, until onions begin to caramelize. Add carrots and another pinch of salt and sauté for 5 minutes, until carrots are cooked but have a slight bite. Stir in garlic and the havij spice mix and cook for 5 minutes until fragrant. Add sour cherries and enough water to cover. Bring to a boil, then reduce heat to medium-low and simmer for 15 minutes, or until reduced by half.

Serve stew alongside basmati rice and salad.

2½ cups heavy cream

2 cups whole or 2% milk

1 tsp vanilla extract

½ tsp ground saffron

6 egg yolks

2 cups sugar

1½ cups unsalted pistachio nuts, coarsely ground, plus extra for garnish

3 Tbsp rosewater

Pinch of salt

Persian Gelato (Bastani)

SERVES 4 This gelato serves as the base for Fooq's Persian sundae, which is topped with sesame paste halvah, crushed pistachios, pomegranate molasses, and sticky strips of Medjool dates. Feel free to give your scoops the royal treatment as well, or just enjoy them on their own, with their distinctly Persian saffron-tinged base.

Bring cream and milk to a boil in a medium saucepan over medium-high heat, stirring frequently to prevent scorching. Add vanilla and saffron, reduce heat to low, and cook for another 3 minutes. Remove from heat.

In a separate bowl, beat egg yolks and sugar until smooth and frothy. Ladle ¼ cup of the hot milk into the bowl and stir to bring eggs up to temperature. Carefully and slowly, pour egg mixture into the pan of hot milk, whisking continuously to ensure even heat distribution.

Heat mixture over low heat and use a wooden spoon to stir continuously for 3 minutes, or until thick enough to coat a spoon. Pour mixture into a bowl and refrigerate for 1 hour, until it is chilled and has the consistency of a loose pudding.

Stir in pistachios and rosewater. Churn in an ice cream maker, following the manufacturer's instructions. (Alternatively, pour mixture into a shallow pan and place in the freezer for an hour. Vigorously stir every 20 minutes or so to break up the ice crystals, until mixture is homogeneous and frozen.)

Scoop into small bowls and top with additional chopped pistachios if desired.

HAKKASAN

JIAN HENG (KENNY) LOO
chef de cuisine

In 2007, Hakkasan opened their first U.S. location at the famed Fontainebleau hotel, which was fresh off a multimillion-dollar refresh and set to make a splashy re-entrance into the Miami scene. Restaurateur Alan Yau, the mastermind behind the Michelin-starred restaurant's London base, showed Brits how to do upscale Asian and since introducing the concept to this side of the Atlantic, the AAA Four Diamond award-winning modern Chinese restaurant has become a fixture of the Miami dining landscape (and is one of twelve worldwide locations).

Make no mistake: this is elevated dining. The dark and seductive dining room overlooks the ocean but all attention is focused indoors, on the maze-like warren of carved wood alcoves, each illuminated by Chinese lanterns and fitted with turquoise leather seating. Double-height doors, black lacquered latticework, and teak panels of decorative motifs work together with dramatic effect, giving the space a "Shanghai supper club meets Mad Max" feel.

It's a perfect backdrop to a sophisticated feast. Jasmine tea–smoked ribs, crispy almond-pear prawns (page 84), and roasted silver cod in Chinese honey and champagne are skillfully executed. This is authentic Chinese cooking from the mainland, highlighted with Cantonese specialties such as dim sum and wok-fired dishes like stir-fried shredded beef in honey.

Chef de Cuisine Jian Heng (Kenny) Loo presides over a gleaming open kitchen featuring a squadron of white-jacketed chefs toiling over woks blasted by flames. Yet despite all the clanging, the kitchen excels at the small and delicate, such as the shrimp and Chinese chive dumplings, each doughy parcel accented with a goji berry. It's what makes their dim sum lunch one of the most popular in town, and the perfect place to satisfy your Chinese food cravings.

FACING Crispy Spiced Prawns with Asian Pear and Almonds and Crispy Orange Chicken

CHILI-MAYO SAUCE

⅓ cup mayonnaise

¼ cup spicy chili sauce

1 Tbsp condensed milk

½ Tbsp lemon juice

1 tsp confectioners' sugar

½ tsp dried mint

¼ tsp chili powder

CRISPY PRAWNS

1 lb prawns, peeled and deveined

1 tsp salt

1 tsp white pepper

1 egg, beaten

½ cup potato starch

½ cup canola oil

ASSEMBLY

1 English cucumber, thinly sliced

¼ cup diced Asian pear

¼ cup sliced almonds

Pinch of black sesame seeds

Microgreens, for garnish

Crispy Spiced Prawns with Asian Pear and Almonds

SERVES 2 TO 3 This dish hits all the right notes. A spicy mayo sauce giving the sweet prawns a fiery coating and the almonds add textural crunch, while the pear's sweetness tempers the spice.

CHILI-MAYO SAUCE In a bowl, combine all ingredients together. Cover and set aside.

CRISPY PRAWNS Season prawns with salt and pepper.

Place egg and potato starch in separate bowls. Dip each prawn in the egg, then dredge in potato starch.

Heat oil in a deep, heavy skillet over medium-high heat. Gently lower prawns and fry for 5 minutes, or until golden brown. Using a slotted spoon, transfer prawns to a paper towel–lined plate.

Place prawns in the bowl of chili mayo and toss to coat each piece.

ASSEMBLY Arrange cucumber slices on a large platter. Place prawns on top and garnish with Asian pear, almonds, sesame seeds, and microgreens.

CHICKEN

3 boneless, skinless
chicken breasts

1 tsp salt

1 tsp white pepper

1 Tbsp baking powder

1 Tbsp potato starch

1 Tbsp all-purpose flour

½ Tbsp custard powder

1 egg, beaten

½ cup canola oil

ORANGE SAUCE

2 tsp custard powder

Pinch of salt

Pinch of sugar

Juice of 3 oranges

1 tsp rice vinegar

ASSEMBLY

1 banana leaf, to serve

1 orange, thinly sliced

Pinch of black sesame
seeds

Grated zest of 1 orange

Crispy Orange Chicken

SERVES 3 A modern spin on the Chinese restaurant classic, this chicken has a light breading and a bright flavor from freshly squeezed orange juice. It's best served with rice and vibrant greens.

CHICKEN Season chicken with salt and pepper and set aside.

In a shallow dish, combine baking powder, potato starch, flour, and custard powder. Put egg in a separate dish. Dip chicken in egg, then dredge in the flour mixture.

Heat oil in a large skillet over medium-high heat. Add chicken and fry for 8 to 10 minutes, until golden brown. Turn and cook on the other side for another 8 to 10 minutes, until golden. Transfer chicken to a paper towel–lined plate.

ORANGE SAUCE In a saucepan, combine all ingredients and bring to a boil over high heat. Boil for 3 minutes, then turn off heat and set aside.

ASSEMBLY Set the banana leaf on a platter. Cut chicken into strips and arrange on the platter with slices of orange between the strips. Pour orange sauce on top. Garnish with sesame seeds and grated orange zest.

JAYA AT THE SETAI

VIJAYUDU VEENA
executive chef

It's all too fitting that the Sanskrit translation of the word *jaya* is "victory" since this posh eatery at The Setai has managed a feat that so many have tried and very few have succeeded at: churning out good Southeast Asian food in South Beach. It's also fitting that the restaurant has been helmed for over a decade by Chef Vijay Veena, who learned to cook the flavors of his native Hyderabad in India at his father's restaurant, Chakram, which served regional culinary specialties. This experience ignited a love of flavors and spices that eventually led Veena to culinary school in Switzerland and then to a spot in the coveted kitchen that serves the temple-like dining room of The Setai. Jaya's menu follows the spice trail from India to other Asian regions including China, Thailand, Japan, Bali, and Korea.

"Indian cuisine is rich with spices," says Veena. "My upbringing has heavily influenced my cooking, giving my style of cuisine a very distinctive flavor palate for diners in the United States. While most of my colleagues consider salt their 'go-to' ingredient, I reach for cumin, saffron, and curry."

And oh, that courtyard. I often find myself staking out one of the pods that flank the serenity pond in the hotel's tree-lined atrium to feast on the eclectic dishes that make Jaya such a favorite among locals. Dishes such as Peking duck with all the fixings, steamed scallop and shrimp dumplings topped with truffle cream and shaved truffles, chicken tikka from the tandoor oven, and of course those authentic Indian and Thai curries. A night dining on those colorful dishes brimming with spices and flavors will make you feel pampered, in the best possible way.

TAMARIND SAUCE

1 Tbsp canola oil

2 shallots, chopped

2 stalks lemongrass, chopped

10 red Thai chiles, chopped

¼ cup white wine

1 Tbsp red wine vinegar

½ cup tamarind concentrate (see Note)

¼ cup oyster sauce

⅓ cup cane sugar

¼ cup soy sauce

GRILLED SNAPPER

4 (6-oz) skinless snapper fillets, pin bones removed

2 Tbsp canola oil

Salt and black pepper

ASSEMBLY

2 red Thai chiles, chopped, seeded, and deveined

Chopped cilantro

Jasmine rice, to serve

Grilled Snapper with Tamarind Sauce

SERVES 4 Chef Vijay Veena's signature dish sees grilled fish ramped up with a complex sweet-sour sauce of fiery chiles, tamarind, and sharp vinegar. Tamarind, sometimes referred to as the Indian date, can be sweet, tart, and sour all at once, so a little goes a very long way. If you can't find snapper, feel free to use another white fish such as cod or sole.

TAMARIND SAUCE Heat oil in a large skillet over medium heat. Add shallots and sauté for 5 to 7 minutes, until translucent. Add lemongrass and chiles and sauté for another 2 minutes. Stir in wine and vinegar and cook for another 5 minutes, until reduced by a quarter.

Stir in tamarind concentrate, oyster sauce, sugar, and soy sauce and cook for another 5 to 7 minutes, until the sauce is thick enough to coat a spoon. Reduce heat to low and keep warm until needed.

GRILLED SNAPPER Preheat grill to high heat.

Brush fillets with oil, then season with salt and pepper. Grill for 5 to 6 minutes on each side, until cooked through.

ASSEMBLY Transfer fish to a serving platter, pour the tamarind sauce overtop, and garnish with chiles and cilantro. Serve immediately with rice.

NOTE Tamarind concentrate is a thick, dark paste that is mildly sweet. It can be found online or at Caribbean or Indian grocers.

CURRY PASTE

10 cloves garlic

4 jalapeños, chopped

2 stalks lemongrass, chopped

1 green bell pepper, seeded and deveined

Bunch of cilantro

1 cup chopped spinach

¼ cup chopped galangal

THAI GREEN CURRY

¼ cup canola oil

1 cup Curry Paste (see here)

2 (13½-oz) cans coconut milk

1 Tbsp palm sugar or brown sugar

Pinch of salt

5 multicolored bell peppers, seeded, deveined, and sliced

4 fingerling potatoes, halved

1 Thai eggplant, cut into large chunks

½ cup bamboo shoots

¼ cup Thai basil

Sliced jalapeño peppers, for garnish

Cilantro leaves, for garnish

Jasmine rice, to serve

Thai Green Curry

SERVES 8 Thai green curry—my favorite dish at Jaya—is pure comfort food. The mildly spicy sauce is made rich with coconut milk and loaded with tender vegetables. Best of all, its sophisticated curry base is prepared without fish sauce, making this a super easy, vegan-friendly dish.

CURRY PASTE Combine all ingredients in a food processor and blend into a fine paste.

THAI GREEN CURRY Heat oil in a large saucepan over medium heat. Add curry paste and cook for 3 to 5 minutes, until fragrant. Add coconut milk, reduce to low heat, and cook for another 5 to 7 minutes. Stir in sugar and season with salt.

Add bell peppers, potatoes, eggplant, bamboo shoots, and Thai basil and cook for 10 to 12 minutes, until vegetables are tender. Ladle curry into bowls, garnish with jalapeño peppers and cilantro, and serve with rice.

THE JIM AND NEESIE

DANIEL ROY
executive chef

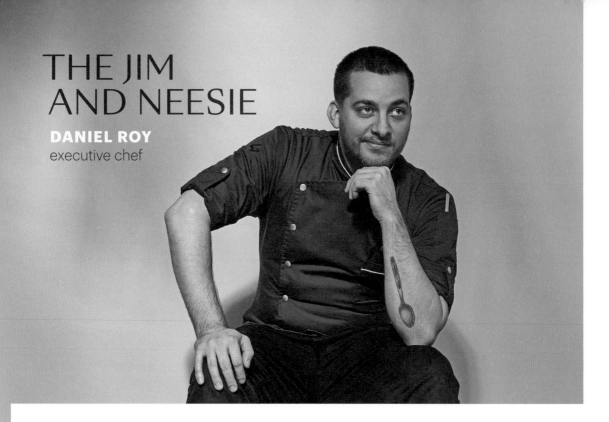

When the London-based Generator Hostel brand was looking to launch their first American outpost in Miami, they looked to young chef Daniel Roy to head up their culinary operations for that first flagship and all subsequent U.S. locations. Having worked with top toque Jeremy Ford at Stubborn Seed and Jean-Georges Vongerichten's Matador Room, Roy was well-versed in the style of fine dining and molecular gastronomy that often comes with five-star menus. But for this project, housed in a very trend-setting and sophisticated hostel (let's be honest, it feels more like a boutique hotel), he went for a more relaxed approach.

The restaurant's name and inspiration come from an imagined older couple who are living their best lives and hosting fun, eclectic dinner parties in their dimly lit and intimate apartment. The restaurant's dining room flanking the hostel's refurbished lobby, which still has traces of its original Art Deco design, is outfitted in quirky touches like brick walls, light

fixtures made of wine bottles, and framed family photos. Funky floor tiles and greenery add color while a well-stocked bar churns out craft cocktails and drinks served tableside.

But while The Jim and Neesie has a cozy and relatively casual look, the dishes are far more complex. Charred asparagus comes topped with a crispy poached truffle egg, the obligatory kale salad gains depth with sherry trumpet mushrooms and spiced pecans, and charred Romanesco comes with a celery leaf pesto (page 92). Heartier appetites can be satisfied by a burger topped with Grafton white cheddar, seared prawns with salsa verde, and *cacio e pepe* (a pasta with salt, freshly ground black pepper, and Parmesan) topped with shaved truffle and lemon zest. Together the dishes make up the kind of delicious dinner party you wish would never end.

FACING Charred Romanesco with Celery Leaf Pesto and Harissa and Jim's Yellow Fedora

90

CELERY LEAF PESTO

1 cup packed celery leaves

½ cup Italian parsley

¼ cup grated Parmesan

¼ cup toasted pepitas

2 Tbsp lemon juice

1 tsp grated lemon zest

¼ cup extra-virgin olive oil

Salt and black pepper

HARISSA

2 jalapeños, seeded

2 cloves garlic

1 cup chopped piquillo peppers or roasted red bell peppers

2 Tbsp sambal oelek

1 Tbsp ground cumin

1 Tbsp ground coriander

1 Tbsp salt, plus extra to taste

2 Tbsp lemon juice

½ cup grapeseed oil

ROMANESCO

1 (1-lb) head Romanesco

¼ cup extra-virgin olive oil

Salt and black pepper

ASSEMBLY

½ cup Harissa (see here)

¼ cup feta cheese

Juice of 1 lemon

Pinch of salt

1 Tbsp chopped cilantro

1 Tbsp torn basil leaves

1 Tbsp chopped Italian parsley

Charred Romanesco with Celery Leaf Pesto and Harissa

SERVES 2 TO 4 Romanesco is broccoli's sexier cousin, with a dense, heavy head covered in spiraling points and a vibrant green color. In this iteration, Chef Daniel Roy gives the veggie a flavor-packed harissa base and a celery leaf pesto that will have you asking for seconds.

CELERY LEAF PESTO In a food processor, combine celery leaves, parsley, Parmesan, pepitas, and lemon juice and zest. Process until combined. With the motor still running, slowly pour in oil and process until well incorporated, scraping down sides of the bowl if necessary. Season with salt and pepper and set aside.

HARISSA Combine all ingredients except the oil in a blender and purée. Slowly add the oil and season with salt. (Leftover harissa can be stored in an airtight container in the refrigerator for up to two weeks.)

ROMANESCO Preheat oven to 400°F.

Bring a stockpot of water to a boil. Add Romanesco and cook for 3 to 5 minutes, until a knife can pierce it with little resistance. Drain, then brush oil over Romanesco and season with salt and pepper. Place on a baking sheet and roast for 10 to 12 minutes, until it starts to brown.

ASSEMBLY Warm up harissa in a small saucepan and stir in feta. Transfer mixture to a serving plate. Place Romanesco on top, then drizzle with celery leaf pesto. Sprinkle lemon juice overtop, season with salt, and garnish with herbs.

2 oz rye whiskey

¾ oz lemon juice

¾ oz store-bought demerara syrup

¼ oz yellow chartreuse

4 mint leaves, plus a sprig for garnish

Lime wheel, for garnish

Jim's Yellow Fedora

SERVES 1 Chartreuse—a liquor distilled using 130 natural herbs, spices, and flowers—is generally sipped as a digestif. In this recipe it adds depth to whiskey for a play on the classic green hat cocktail—with a Jim and Neesie spin.

Combine all ingredients except garnishes in a shaker with ice and shake for 15 seconds. Fine-strain into a Collins glass with crushed ice. Garnish with a mint sprig and a lime wheel.

JUVIA/ SUSHI GARAGE

SUNNY OH
executive chef

Executive Chef Sunny Oh can easily straddle the needs of his two restaurants, Juvia and Sushi Garage, having honed his skills at Nobu for years. And he's been around long enough to see the industry evolve. "I have lived in South Florida for more than twenty years, and Miami has unexpectedly transformed into this amazing and culturally diverse city," says Oh. "It's hard to be anywhere else."

Oh's Juvia is an ultrachic open-air penthouse perched atop a Herzog & de Meuron–designed building and boasts compelling views of Miami. (The restaurant won a James Beard award for Outstanding Restaurant Design.) But the real draw is the food, and menu highlights include tuna tataki with white soy dressing and a Scottish salmon-honey-yuzu-mustard *tiradito*.

Sushi Garage, on the other hand, is a cavernous space—a former auto body shop—outfitted with blond wood tables, circular booths on elevated platforms, and fish sculptures dangling from the ceiling. Here, diners feast on popular Japanese dishes, and rolls run the gamut from spicy tuna to unagi with white pepper–rosemary aioli to hamachi, scallion, and micro cilantro (page 96).

The restaurants appeal to locals and out-of-towners alike. "Miami has built a solid selection of quality of restaurants, and it's drawing the attention of the world," says Oh. While Juvia and Sushi Garage both boast stunning IG-worthy interiors, Oh's global approach and penchant for high-end sushi and composed Asian dishes bring people back.

SEA BASS

2 Tbsp vegetable oil

4 (7-oz) fillets Chilean
sea bass

Salt and black pepper

SAUCE

1 cup (2 sticks) butter

6 Tbsp demi-glace
(see Note)

¼ cup black garlic purée
(see Note)

½ cup soy sauce

Handful of basil leaves,
chopped

ASSEMBLY

4 heads baby bok choy

1 Tbsp vegetable oil

4 shiitake mushrooms

2 English cucumbers,
thinly sliced with a
mandoline

4 breakfast radishes, thinly
sliced with a mandoline

1 cup micro arugula,
for garnish

Chilean Sea Bass with Brown Butter–Soy Sauce

SERVES 4 Unbeknownst to most people, Chilean sea bass is not in fact a sea bass but a Patagonian toothfish that was renamed to appeal to the market. In this recipe, the delicious pan-seared fish is served with bok choy, fresh cucumbers and radishes, and a superb butter-soy reduction.

SEA BASS Preheat oven to 450°F.

Heat oil in a large ovenproof skillet over medium-high heat. Season sea bass with salt and pepper. Add to pan and pan-sear for 1 to 2 minutes per side, until golden. Place skillet in the oven for 5 minutes, until the fish is fully cooked.

SAUCE Heat a small saucepan over high heat. Melt butter and cook for 2 to 3 minutes, until it starts to brown. Add demi-glace and black garlic purée and boil for 3 minutes, until thickened. Lower heat to medium-high, add soy sauce and basil, and cook for another 8 to 10 minutes, until reduced by half.

ASSEMBLY Bring a medium saucepan of water to a boil. Add bok choy and blanch for 1 minute. Drain, then plunge into a bowl of ice water. Cut the bok choy in half and set aside.

Heat oil in a skillet over medium-high heat. Add bok choy and shiitakes and sauté for 8 to 10 minutes, until cooked through.

Arrange cucumber and radish slices on each plate. Add the bok choy and shiitakes, then position the sea bass on top. Drizzle with sauce and garnish with micro arugula.

NOTE *Demi-glace*, made from veal stock, is a gourmet item that can be found at fine food stores or online.

Black garlic purée is a condiment used in Asian cooking. It can be purchased at most Asian markets or online.

SUSHI RICE

1 cup red or white
Japanese vinegar

3 Tbsp sugar

Pinch of salt

3 cups uncooked
sushi rice

HAMACHI CILANTRO ROLLS

12 oz sushi-grade hamachi
(yellowtail), finely
chopped

Bunch of scallions, green
parts only, thinly sliced

1 cup micro cilantro

½ cup yuzu juice

½ cup soy sauce

4 sheets nori

¼ cup sesame seeds,
toasted

1 Tbsp pea shoots

1 Tbsp pickled ginger

1 tsp wasabi paste

Hamachi Cilantro Rolls

MAKES 4 ROLLS Preparing your own sushi at home may seem intimidating, but once you get the hang of it, the technique is fairly easy. Quality is the key concern, and it's essential to buy sushi-grade fish. You'll also want to avoid overworking the rice: sushi rice needs air to make good sushi. And always dip your knife in a bowl of water to ensure clean slices when you cut your maki.

SUSHI RICE In a small bowl, combine vinegar, sugar, and salt.

In a rice cooker, combine rice, vinegar mixture, and 4 cups of water. Cook, then set aside to cool.

HAMACHI CILANTRO ROLLS In a bowl, combine hamachi, scallions, and cilantro and gently toss.

In another bowl, combine yuzu juice and soy sauce.

Position a bamboo rolling mat on a cutting board so the bamboo strips are running horizontally to you. Place a sheet of plastic wrap over the bamboo mat, then lay a sheet of nori on top. Spread a thin layer of rice over it, leaving about a ¾-inch space along the top edge so the roll can be sealed. Scatter sesame seeds overtop.

Using the plastic wrap, flip the nori and rice over, then place a quarter of the hamachi mixture onto the nori in a horizontal line, close to the bottom of the sheet. Gently lift the bottom of the mat up and over so the rice and nori form a roll around the filling. As you continue to pull the mat, press and shape the roll into a tube, using pressure to create a firm roll. Repeat to make the other three rolls.

Cut each hamachi cilantro roll into 8 slices and garnish with pea shoots. Serve immediately with the pickled ginger, wasabi, and yuzu-soy dipping sauce on the side.

KIKI ON THE RIVER

STEVE RHEE
executive chef

With the opening of Kiki on the River in 2017, the laid-back luxury of the Greek islands arrived on the once-gritty banks of Miami's namesake river, bringing this sprawling beauty that has stolen the hearts of socialites, discerning food lovers, and celebrities alike. Opened by hospitality impresarios looking to bring a bit of South Beach energy to the waterfront, it mixes breezy elegance with clean, fresh, and classic flavors from the Aegean to spectacular effect.

The kitchen is helmed by Executive Chef Steve Rhee, an industry veteran who opened Estiatorio Milos in Miami Beach and served three years as sous chef at the Las Vegas outpost. Rhee's creative yet approachable dishes reflect the bounty of seafood that comes from the Mediterranean as well as an array of meats prepared simply on the grill. Everything is made in-house and many of the fresh ingredients—including the spices, herbs, and olive oil—come directly from Greece.

Reserve one of the elevated dining cabanas on Kiki's outdoor terrace draped in ivy vines and colorful bougainvillea and take in river views as you feast on a welcoming trio of spreads or a watermelon and feta salad that keeps its promise of crunch and punch. As expected, fish is a focal point, both on the menu and in the dining room, where waiters regularly pull up trolleys of salt-crusted Mediterranean branzino (or *lavraki*) that are served tableside. Dessert might seem impossible at the end of such a repast, but even the fullest of bellies will make room for the Greek yogurt with thyme honey and toasted walnuts. By the end of the meal, you will have seen the twinkle of the Aegean beyond the lights of downtown Miami.

LADOLEMONO SAUCE

1 cup lemon juice

1 cup extra-virgin olive oil

2 Tbsp dried Greek oregano

1 tsp sea salt

FRIED CAPERS

1 cup capers

½ cup canola oil

OCTOPUS

4 lbs whole octopus

2 carrots, cut diagonally

2 stalks celery, cut diagonally

2 yellow Spanish onions, chopped

1 red onion, thinly sliced

Bunch of Italian parsley

Bunch of thyme

½ cup capers

6 bay leaves

2 Tbsp black peppercorns

2 Tbsp white peppercorns

2 Tbsp coriander seeds

4 cups canola oil, plus extra for brushing

1 cup red wine vinegar

ASSEMBLY

½ cup Ladolemono Sauce (see here)

2 Tbsp Fried Capers (see here)

Sliced red onions

Chopped Italian parsley

Grilled Octopus

SERVES 6 Every satisfying Greek meal should include octopus and the starter served at Kiki's is as good as it gets in evoking an authentic Greek island feast. The lemon-infused *ladolemono* sauce adds a welcome citrusy element that cloaks each bite with brightness.

LADOLEMONO SAUCE In a blender, combine all ingredients and mix well. Cover and set aside.

FRIED CAPERS Rinse capers under cold running water, until the concentrated saltiness is rinsed off. Transfer capers to a paper towel–lined plate to dry.

Heat oil in a skillet over high heat. Add capers and flash-fry for 2 minutes. Remove from heat and set on paper towel–lined plate to dry.

OCTOPUS Preheat oven to 450°F.

Using a mallet or the end of a rolling pin, gently pound out octopus tentacles to tenderize. Rinse octopus under cold running water, then use a sharp knife to remove head and beak. Discard.

Place octopus in a large roasting pan. Add the remaining ingredients, ensuring that the tentacles are completely submerged. Roast for 1 hour, until cooked through and tender.

Using a slotted spoon, transfer octopus to a wire rack and set aside to cool to room temperature.

Preheat grill to high heat and brush with oil. Add tentacles and cook for 4 minutes on each side, until charred all over. Remove immediately and cut into bite-sized chunks.

ASSEMBLY Place octopus in a serving bowl. Add ladolemono sauce and fried capers and toss. Scatter onions on top and garnish with parsley.

TUNA

¼ lb center-cut tuna, chopped

10 cilantro leaves

1 Tbsp finely chopped English cucumber

1 Tbsp kalamata olives

1 Tbsp extra-virgin olive oil

1 tsp sea salt

AVOCADO PURÉE

2 Hass avocados

1 cup chopped cilantro

¼ cup lime juice

1 Tbsp lemon juice

1 Tbsp salt

½ Tbsp sugar

SAMBAL SAUCE

2 Tbsp extra-virgin olive oil

1 red bell pepper, seeded, deveined, and finely chopped

1 white onion, finely chopped (1 cup)

3 cloves garlic, finely chopped

1 Tbsp lime juice

1 tsp chili flakes

1 tsp salt

1 tsp sugar

ASSEMBLY

2 Tbsp Sambal Sauce (see here)

Tuna (see here)

Microgreens, to serve

Pita chips, to serve

Tuna Tartare

SERVES 2 Greek ingredients such as kalamata olives give a welcome briny kick to Chef Rhee's version of this classic dish. It makes for an elegant starter for a light meal focused on seafood and spreads.

TUNA Mix all ingredients together in a bowl. Set aside.

AVOCADO PURÉE Blend all ingredients in a blender until smooth. Set aside.

SAMBAL SAUCE Heat oil in a skillet over medium heat. Add pepper, onion, and garlic and sauté for 4 minutes, until tender. Set aside to cool to room temperature.

Transfer mixture to a blender, add remaining ingredients, and blend until smooth. Set aside.

ASSEMBLY Add 2 tablespoons sambal sauce to the tuna mixture and gently toss to coat.

Place avocado purée in a chilled bowl and spoon the tuna mixture on top. Serve with microgreens and pita chips.

KOMODO

DAVID GRUTMAN
owner

Komodo was nightlife guru David Grutman's first foray into the restaurant business back in 2015. It seems quaint now to look back at a time when the gregarious Grutman was just dipping his toe in the tumultuous waters of the restaurant world. Today, as the proprietor of Groot Hospitality, he has a growing empire of five restaurants, with more to come.

Komodo is a fixture on the Miami dining scene, regarded as one of the city's top twenty highest-grossing independent restaurants (with annual sales at around $22 million). The restaurant also exemplifies the "clubstaurant" model, being a venue that straddles the line between restaurant and nightclub: a booming sound system, a sprawling space, and an embracing of late-night hedonism are all part of the show.

The flashy cathedral of Asian cooking spans three floors and getting reservations for one of its 300 seats on a weekend is nearly impossible. And on any given night, you'll find Grutman hosting one of his many famous DJ friends, reality-show stars, or pop-music icons. Given all this fanfare, you might expect the food to be an afterthought, but the menu is equally impressive.

The food is pan-Asian with Japanese, Chinese, and Thai influences and plenty of high-roller touches such as black truffles and lobster. You'll find Korean fried chicken alongside Thai beef jerky and miso sea bass skewers, as well as comforting pastrami egg rolls, stuffed with cabbage and served with spicy mustard, inspired by Grutman's own family recipe.

Despite the bling and hype, it's easy to see why the restaurant does well and often serves upwards of a thousand diners on busy nights. With such a varied menu, it's truly a something-for-everyone eatery and consistently delicious enough to wow even the most demanding diners.

FACING Maine Lobster and Golden Geisha

YUZU BROWN BUTTER

1½ cups (3 sticks) cold
   butter (divided)
2 cups sake
3 Tbsp yuzu juice
Salt, to taste

MAINE LOBSTER

1 (2½-lb) live Maine lobster
1 cup all-purpose flour
¼ cup onion salt
2 Tbsp paprika
2 Tbsp cayenne
2 Tbsp garlic salt
2 Tbsp canola oil
3 chives, for garnish
Seared lemon wedges,
   to serve

Maine Lobster

SERVES 2 Maine lobster, prized for its tender texture and sweet flavor, is undoubtedly the star of this dish, but the seasoned flour that coats the crustacean's delectable meat plays a supporting role that makes it addictive. Fans of Komodo will take delight in re-creating this signature lobster dish with yuzu brown butter and seared lemon.

YUZU BROWN BUTTER Melt ½ cup butter in a small saucepan over medium-low heat and cook for 5 minutes, until nutty brown. Reserve ¼ cup.

Heat sake in another small saucepan over medium-high heat for 7 to 10 minutes, until reduced to a quarter. Add ¼ cup brown butter and yuzu juice and cook for another 5 minutes, or until reduced by half. Cut the remaining 1 cup butter into ½-inch pieces and add to pan. Stir until fully melted, then season with salt. Set aside.

MAINE LOBSTER Preheat oven to 400°F.

Bring a stockpot of salted water to a boil. Carefully lower lobster into the water and boil for 5 minutes, Drain, then plunge in a bowl of ice-cold water.

Combine the flour and spices in a shallow bowl. Split the lobster in half lengthwise and dredge in the seasoning mixture. Shake off excess.

Heat oil in a large ovenproof skillet over high heat. Add lobster halves and pan-sear, flesh-side down, for 1 minute. Turn over and sear for another minute. Place skillet in the oven and roast for 5 minutes to finish.

Arrange both lobster halves on a large serving platter, garnish with chives, and serve with seared lemon wedges and yuzu brown butter.

8 raspberries
1½ oz Tito's vodka
⅔ oz apple juice
⅔ oz aloe vera water
⅓ oz lemon juice
Gold leaf flakes,
    for garnish

Golden Geisha

SERVES 1 This refreshing cocktail is deceptively easy to prepare and heightened to a luxe level with edible gold leaf flakes, which can be purchased from specialty grocers or online sources.

Muddle raspberries in a shaker, then add the remaining ingredients and ice. Shake, then drain twice into a coupe glass. Garnish with gold leaf flakes.

KYU

STEVEN HAIGH
owner

MICHAEL LEWIS
owner and executive chef

When two Zuma alums decided to strike out on their own and open a restaurant in Wynwood in 2016, the Miami food world was skeptical. True, they had both earned their chops working at the Asian mega-restaurant—Chef Michael Lewis spent time in top kitchens from Hong Kong to Dubai working under chefs like Jean-Georges Vongerichten, and Steven Haigh was probably one of the best general managers in the city—but at the time, Wynwood was mostly comprised of galleries in graffiti-clad ware-houses along gritty streets.

But doubts were quickly laid to rest soon after opening as KYU became one of the hottest restaurants in town, where well-heeled patrons could expect a weeks-long waiting list for a coveted table during prime dinner hours.

General manager Haigh makes sure front of the house runs smoothly, with well-trained and attentive servers in jeans and bib aprons making the rounds, eager to describe chef's latest special or rhapsodize about the life-changing roasted cauliflower with goat cheese and shishito-herb vinaigrette (page 110). And yes, it really is *that* good.

This Asian barbecue place with the curious name (it's pronounced "q") and a menu divided into categories with names like "snacky snacks" and "crispy-crunchy" has won over everyone from winter snowbirds to locals, who pack the bar at happy hour or come time and again for the smoked Wagyu beef brisket. But despite the hard-to-get reservations and critically lauded food, KYU is a homey, unpretentious space with polished concrete floors and blond wood tables, where nearly every table will finish a meal with their famous coconut cake: a glorious four-layer tower of coconut shavings and cream, courtesy of Lewis's mother's recipe.

SHISHITO-HERB VINAIGRETTE

1 cup grapeseed oil

½ cup shishito peppers

¼ cup Italian parsley leaves

¼ cup culantro leaves (see Note)

2 Tbsp mint leaves

½ cup pickled jalapeños

¼ cup pickled jalapeño juice

2 Tbsp sudachi juice (see Note)

½ Tbsp salt

Roasted Cauliflower with Goat Cheese and Shishito-Herb Vinaigrette

SERVES 2 TO 4 (AS A SIDE) The team at KYU sells over hundred portions of cauliflower a day and it's easy to see why. The vibrant chile vinaigrette packs a wallop of herby flavor that complements the meatiness of the florets, while the tart goat cheese ties it all together with a welcome creaminess.

SHISHITO-HERB VINAIGRETTE Heat oil to 350°F in a saucepan over high heat. Add shishito peppers and deep-fry for 2 to 3 minutes, until tender. Transfer to a paper towel–lined plate and set aside to cool. Remove stems. Reserve the oil.

Bring water to a boil in a small saucepan. Add parsley, culantro, and mint and blanch for 15 seconds. Transfer herbs to a bowl of ice water to cool, then drain and dry. (This gives the dressing its vibrant green color.)

Transfer peppers, herbs, and remaining ingredients to a blender and purée until smooth. Gradually add the reserved oil and purée until blended. Set aside to cool. (Leftover vinaigrette can be stored in an airtight container in the refrigerator for up to two days.)

NOTE Culantro is an herb with serrated leaves and the appearance of long-leafed lettuce. It can be substituted with cilantro.

Sudachi juice is derived from a Japanese citrus fruit and adds a sour citrus flavor with notes of fresh ginger, and is used as a food flavoring in place of vinegar. It is available from online retailers.

GOAT CHEESE

½ cup soft goat cheese, such as Coach Farm

¼ cup buttermilk

½ tsp salt

¼ tsp cayenne powder

ROASTED CAULIFLOWER

⅓ cup salt

1 large head cauliflower

¼ cup extra-virgin olive oil, plus extra for brushing

Salt and black pepper

ASSEMBLY

2 tsp extra-virgin olive oil

2 shiso leaves, cut into strips

½ piece myoga or a slice of ginger, cut into matchsticks (see Note)

GOAT CHEESE In a bowl, combine all ingredients using a fork.

ROASTED CAULIFLOWER Preheat oven to 500°F.

Bring water and salt to a boil in a stockpot. Add cauliflower and cook for 3 minutes. Drain.

Rub cauliflower with oil and season with salt and pepper. Place on a rack-lined roasting pan and roast for 10 minutes. Remove, then brush once more with oil if needed. Cook for another 7 minutes, until lightly browned.

ASSEMBLY Using ¼ cup of the shishito-herb vinaigrette, draw a circle slightly larger than the head of cauliflower on a large plate. (Using a squeeze bottle makes this easier!)

Place 3 tablespoons of goat cheese in the center of the plate. Set cauliflower on top. Finish with a drizzle of olive oil and garnish with shiso and myoga.

NOTE Myoga is a Japanese ginger, and unlike ginger root, only the buds and shoots are used for cooking. It can be found at Japanese or Asian grocers, or you can substitute with regular ginger.

MISO BUTTER

1½ Tbsp sake

1½ Tbsp mirin

1 Tbsp sugar

3 Tbsp saikyo miso
(see Note)

3 Tbsp shiro miso
(see Note)

1½ cups (3 sticks) butter,
at room temperature

RED SNAPPER

4 (3½-oz) fresh Florida
red snapper fillets or any
flaky white fish, skinless

Salt, to taste

2 cups Miso Butter
(see here)

ASSEMBLY

1 cup celery leaves

1 cup shiso or mint leaves

1 cup Thai basil leaves

½ cup ponzu dressing or
lemon vinaigrette

1 Tbsp miso butter

1 tsp shredded radish

Florida Red Snapper

SERVES 4 "I created the snapper dish as a local and more sustainable version of a traditional black cod miso dish," explains Chef Michael Lewis. "We're not picky on subspecies or size, either. If the local boats are catching it at the moment because it's plentiful, that is what I want."

MISO BUTTER In a small saucepan, combine sake and mirin and cook over medium heat for 2 minutes, until the alcohol is burned off. Stir in sugar until dissolved. Set aside to cool, then stir in both misos.

In a stand mixer fitted with the whisk attachment, whip butter. Slowly add miso mixture and mix until incorporated. Set aside.

NOTE Saikyo miso is a pale, mild miso from Kyoto, Japan. Because of its low sodium content, it can be used in a variety of sweet and savory dishes. Shiro miso is a white miso made with fermented soy beans and rice. Both can be found in Japanese supermarkets.

RED SNAPPER Preheat oven to 400°F.

Season fillets with salt.

Heat miso butter in an ovenproof skillet over medium heat, until butter turns foamy. Add fillets, presentation-side down, and cook for 1 minute, untouched. Put the skillet into the oven and bake for 5 to 10 minutes, until the internal temperature of the fish is 145°F.

ASSEMBLY In a bowl, combine all ingredients and toss gently to mix.

Plate fillets on individual plates and serve with a side of herb salad, miso butter, and shredded radish. Brush fillets with a little extra miso butter, if needed.

LA MAR BY GASTÓN ACURIO

DIEGO OKA
executive chef

Diego Oka is known as the protégé of Chef Gastón Acurio, having worked with the Peruvian celebrity chef since he was eighteen, eventually climbing the ranks to executive chef. But at the helm of the Miami outpost of La Mar since its opening in 2014, Oka has solidified his own reputation as a rising culinary star in our city. With his signature black-framed glasses and warm smile (and sometimes trucker hat), Oka's humble demeanor belies a terrific talent that isn't afraid to toggle between elaborate and straightforward impulses, tweaking classics with his own unique spin.

Acurio and Oka designed the menu to be traditional Peruvian at its core with an emphasis on cebiche and *tiraditos* (page 116), the raw or cured sashimi-style fish dishes with punchy colorful sauces made with various peppers and citrus notes. "Certain things on our menu will never change," says Oka. "We will always have a *cebiche classico* and a *lomo*

saltado because those are Peruvian classics." But there's plenty of wiggle room within the expansive menu to change things up. Oka is always looking for new ingredients to fill his mostly traditional, yet slightly experimental, menu. And his food is as beautiful as it is delicious, with colors that mimic Peruvian embroidery—using elements like purple potatoes, beets, edible flowers, and orange and yellow sauces to dazzling effect. With Peru's 4,000 types of potatoes and complex culinary tradition as his palette, Oka is creating some of the most artful food in the city.

BEET CAUSA

1 beet, unpeeled

2 lbs Yukon Gold potatoes, unpeeled

Salt and black pepper, to taste

Juice of 2 lemons

SUNCHOKES TARTARE

1 lb sunchokes, rinsed, scrubbed well, and cut into ½-inch slices

1 Tbsp canola oil, plus extra for drizzling

1½ tsp salt (divided)

Pinch of black pepper

2 Tbsp mayonnaise

1 Tbsp lime juice

½ Tbsp togarashi

ASSEMBLY

1 tsp Osetra caviar (optional)

1 piece gold leaf (optional, see Note)

Mini edible flowers, such as violetas, lobelia, or clavelina

Flor de Papa

SERVES 4 Mashed potatoes are a comfort food in many cultures, and it's no different in Peru. Instead of using milk or butter, the Peruvian version of mashed potatoes is enhanced with lemon juice and salt, and in this case—beets. Served cold and topped with a sunchoke salad, it makes for a light and refreshing appetizer on a summer day.

BEET CAUSA Put beet in a small saucepan, fill with enough water to cover, and boil gently over medium heat for 25 minutes, until cooked through. Drain and set aside.

Put potatoes in a saucepan, fill with enough water to cover, and boil gently over medium heat for 25 minutes, until cooked through. Drain, allow to cool slightly, then peel potatoes while still warm. Using a potato ricer or masher, mash potatoes and set aside to cool for 3 minutes. Season with salt, pepper, and lemon juice.

Peel beet, then coarsely chop. Put beet into blender and purée. Add beet to the potato mixture a little at a time (to prevent softening the potato too much) and mix well.

SUNCHOKES TARTARE Preheat oven to 425°F and place a rack in the center position.

In a medium bowl, combine sunchokes, oil, ½ teaspoon salt, and pepper and toss until coated. Place sunchokes, cut-side down, on a baking sheet and roast for 9 to 11 minutes. Flip and cook for another 9 to 11 minutes, until lightly caramelized and fork tender. Drizzle with oil to prevent any sticking.

Transfer sunchokes to a bowl and mix with mayonnaise, lime juice, the remaining 1 teaspoon salt, and togarashi until fully coated. Set aside.

ASSEMBLY Spoon beet causa into a mound on a serving plate. Top with sunchokes, caviar and gold leaf, if using, and edible flowers.

NOTE Edible gold leaf can be purchased from specialty grocers or online sources.

PARMESAN CREAM

1 Tbsp butter

1½ Tbsp all-purpose flour

½ cup milk

½ cup grated Parmesan

LECHE DE TIGRE BACHICHE

½ cup leche de tigre sauce (available at most Latin American markets)

Juice of 1 lime

¾ cup Parmesan Cream (see here)

½ Tbsp anchovy paste

TIRADITO

¼ lb fresh white fish, such as cobia or snapper, sliced

1 tsp salt

Squeeze of lime juice

ASSEMBLY

3 Tbsp Leche de Tigre Bachiche (see here)

Parmesan Cream (see here), for drizzling

Squid ink or shrimp crackers

1 tsp basil oil or extra-virgin olive oil

8 store-bought crispy garlic chips (optional), for garnish

Microgreens

1 edible flower, for garnish (optional)

Tiradito Bachiche

SERVES 2 Chef Diego Oka's *tiradito bachiche,* also known as "Italian tiradito," was inspired by his travels in Italy and sees well-aged Parmesan, in addition to traditional *leche de tigre* sauce, in the cream base. Layers of garlic chips and crispy squid ink or shrimp crackers are added for a flavorful accent and textural contrast. Italy meets Peru in just one bite. And you know what? It works.

PARMESAN CREAM Heat butter in a small saucepan over low heat for 5 to 7 minutes, until bubbling. Add flour and whisk energetically, breaking up any lumps and making a smooth paste. Add milk and stir for 10 minutes, until sauce has thickened. Remove from heat and fold in Parmesan until fully melted. Set aside.

LECHE DE TIGRE BACHICHE In a blender, combine leche de tigre and lime juice on low speed. Add Parmesan cream and mix until smooth. Add anchovy paste. Set aside. (Leftover sauce can be saved in the refrigerator for up to five days.)

TIRADITO Season fish with salt and lime juice.

ASSEMBLY Pool leche de tigre bachiche on a cold plate, then arrange fish slices on top. Drizzle with Parmesan cream and garnish with crackers, oil, garlic chips, if using, and microgreens. Serve immediately topped with an edible flower, if using.

LEKU

MIKEL GOIKOLEA
chef

When the Rubell family opened their dazzling eponymous museum in the emerging Alla-pattah neighborhood in 2019 they looked to the northern region of Spain and its storied Basque country cuisine to inspire their restau-rant. Led by a team of hospitality industry veterans, and tapping young chef Mikel Goikolea, Leku was born. A native of the Basque region himself, Goikolea worked in the kitchens of Michelin-starred restaurants in northern Spain before moving to Miami in 2017 and joining forces with Le Basque Catering, a full-service catering and event design company in South Florida, as its consulting chef. The opening of Leku allowed him to honor his heri-tage and share his deep understanding of the traditions of Basque cooking directly with guests in Miami.

An impressive Basque grill is the center-piece of the outdoor area where wood-fired items like family-style portions of milk-fed lamb, organic beef Tomahawk chops, whole local fish, and Maine lobsters are prepared. Other classic Basque dishes include classic *pinxtos*, or tiny tapas, seafood salpicón with tomato emulsion, and of course croquetas made with Iberian ham (page 120).

After perusing the thought-provoking contemporary art on display in the sprawling museum, the warm and inviting atmosphere at Leku beckons with promises of perfectly chilled Txakoli—a slightly sparkling, very dry white wine produced in Basque country—and platters of roasted vegetables, grilled meats, and pristine seafood. Snag a table in the outdoor courtyard with its twinkling lights and mod furniture and settle in for a memorable meal surrounded by art and excellent food.

FACING Ham Croquetas and Beet Tartare Salad

2 sheets gelatin

2 qts warm milk

1 ham bone

½ cup (1 stick) + 1 Tbsp butter

2 Tbsp ham fat

2½ cups all-purpose flour (divided)

6 oz Iberian ham, chopped

Salt and black pepper, to taste

4 eggs, beaten

1½ cups breadcrumbs

Canola oil, for deep-frying

Ham Croquetas

MAKES 36 While the dish originally hails from Spain, ham croquetas has been long regarded as Cuba's national appetizer. The filling for Leku's version is prepared with Iberian ham and a ham bone for maximum flavor, then lightly coated in breadcrumbs and fried to crisp perfection. I dare you to eat just one.

Soak gelatin in a bowl of warm water and set aside.

Pour milk into a saucepan over medium-low heat, add ham bone, and allow to warm for 5 to 7 minutes to infuse.

In a medium saucepan over medium heat, melt butter and ham fat together, then add 1 cup flour and cook for 2 to 3 minutes, until roux is about to change color. Pour the infused milk into the roux and whisk until smooth. Reduce heat to medium-low and cook for 30 minutes, stirring occasionally to prevent the sauce from burning.

Add ham, then season with salt and pepper to taste. Add gelatin and stir until thickened. Set aside to cool.

Put the remaining 1½ cups flour and the eggs and breadcrumbs into three shallow bowls. Using 2 tablespoons, shape the filling into oval-shaped croquetas, then dip in the flour, eggs, and breadcrumbs to create the coating. (If desired, place on a parchment-lined baking sheet, cover with plastic wrap, and freeze until needed.)

Heat oil in a deep fryer or deep saucepan to 350°F over medium-high heat. Working in batches to avoid overcrowding, carefully lower croquetas into the oil and deep-fry for 2 to 4 minutes, until golden brown. Transfer to a paper towel–lined plate to drain. Serve immediately.

BEET EMULSION

¼ cup beet juice

1 egg

1 cup extra-virgin olive oil

Salt, to taste

CHIVE EMULSION

1 cup chopped chives

1 cup extra-virgin olive oil

1 egg

1 Tbsp lemon juice

BEET TARTARE SALAD

1 cooked red beet, cut into
¼-inch cubes (½ cup)

3 Tbsp finely chopped
cantaloupe

1 tsp finely chopped
red onion

1 Tbsp apple cider vinegar

Salt, to taste

2 Tbsp Beet Emulsion
(see here)

1 tsp Chive Emulsion
(see here)

1 tsp capers

Black pepper

Olive oil pearls (such as
Caviaroli), for garnish

Beet Tartare Salad

SERVES 1 TO 2 Beets are finely chopped then combined with cantaloupe and red onion to create this plant-based version of a classic dish. At Leku, the tartare is elegantly served with lamb's lettuce and watercress, then balanced out with a chive emulsion. Finish off the bright dish with decadent olive oil pearls, which are available at specialty stores and online.

BEET EMULSION In a blender, combine all ingredients and mix well.

CHIVE EMULSION In a blender, combine all ingredients and mix well.

BEET TARTARE SALAD In a small bowl, combine beet, cantaloupe, red onion, vinegar, and salt. Add beet emulsion and toss.

Press the beet tartare into a 4-inch ring mold in the center of a serving plate, then remove the mold. Dot chive emulsion on the beet tartare and around the plate, and top with capers and black pepper. Top with olive oil pearls and serve.

LT STEAK & SEAFOOD

LAURENT TOURONDEL
partner

The restaurant at The Betsy Hotel holds a special place in my heart, because it's where I had my last meal before giving birth to my first child—it was a glorious supper of French-influenced steakhouse staples by celebrated chef Laurent Tourondel. (I like to joke it was the Gruyère popovers that kickstarted my labor!)

As anyone who's followed his long and storied career knows, Tourondel has a knack for imbuing old formulas (the steakhouse, the burger joint, farm to table, etc.) with elevated sensibility and style, and this is perfectly exemplified in LT Steak & Seafood. It debuted in 2016 with an updated look and menu (it was formerly known as BLT Steak) that emphasized the bounty of the sea. Sure, the menu features prime steaks and a bevy of delicious sides, but the extensive raw bar, the creative sushi counter, and composed fish dishes such as cobia with Cara Cara orange and toasted

almonds (page 125) are what now add to the culinary fireworks on display.

Lucky for us, Tourondel has entrusted the culinary team at The Betsy Hotel to execute this vision and to bring creativity and leadership to the kitchen, incorporating Latin and Middle Eastern inspiration into high-impact dishes such as chermoula salmon with cumin and preserved lemon. It's powerhouse teams like this that make us happy to dine in South Beach.

4 cups whole milk

4 cups all-purpose flour

1½ Tbsp salt

8 eggs

½ cup finely grated
  Gruyère

½ cup finely grated
  Emmentaler

½ cup finely grated fontina

Gruyère Popovers

MAKES 6 These eggy, puffed-up rolls, which greet every table at LT, fill what is undoubtedly one of the best gratis "bread baskets" in town. Tourondel transforms this French bakery staple into a steakhouse classic—just another reason why this restaurant is a bastion of class on Ocean Drive.

Preheat oven to 350°F. Place a popover pan (or a muffin pan) in the oven to warm up.

Warm milk in a saucepan for 5 minutes over medium-low heat. Turn off heat. Combine flour and salt in a small bowl.

Using an electric mixer, whisk eggs in a bowl for 3 minutes until frothy. Alternate adding warm milk and flour and mixing in. Set aside for 4 minutes, then skim off foam from the top.

In a separate bowl, combine cheeses and mix well.

Take hot popover (or muffin) pan out of the oven and set on the stovetop. Carefully fill the individual tins to the top and top each with 1 tablespoon of cheese mixture. Bake for 50 minutes, until golden and cooked through. Keep the oven door closed while popovers are baking, or they will not rise. Serve hot.

COBIA

2 Tbsp canola oil (divided)

2 heads Treviso or radicchio

Salt

1 (1½-lb) skinless cobia fillet, cut into 4 equal pieces

3 Tbsp butter

Juice of 2 lemons

Extra-virgin olive oil, for drizzling

ASSEMBLY

2 blood oranges, peeled and each cut into 4 rounds

2 Cara Cara oranges, peeled and each cut into 4 rounds

2 navel oranges, peeled and each cut into 4 rounds

½ cup Cerignola olives, pitted and quartered

½ cup sliced almonds, toasted

1 cup watercress

Cobia with Cara Cara Orange

SERVES 4 Despite being known as a steakhouse, the restaurant at The Betsy excels with their fish menu and this cobia dish is a perfect example. The oranges add a wonderful brightness to the delicate fish.

COBIA Heat 1 tablespoon oil in a large skillet over medium-high heat. Season Treviso (or radicchio) with salt, then add to skillet and sear for 1½ minutes on each side. Remove from the pan and set aside.

Heat 1 tablespoon oil in the same skillet over medium-high heat. Season fillets with salt, add to the pan, and cook, untouched, for 3 minutes, until golden. Turn fillets and reduce heat to medium-low. Add butter and baste fish for 1 minute. Transfer to a plate and season each with juice of ½ lemon and oil.

ASSEMBLY Plate 2 rounds of each orange on four plates. Place a fillet on top. Cut each Treviso (or radicchio) in half lengthwise and position next to the fish. Garnish dish with olives, almonds, and watercress. Serve immediately.

MALIBU FARM
MIAMI BEACH

HELENE HENDERSON
founder and chef

Malibu Farm Miami Beach could be perceived as the quintessential Miami restaurant: it overlooks the ocean, boasts a farm-inspired menu of vegetable-focused dishes, and tempts you with promises of lazy weekend lunches followed by strolls on a boardwalk. But in reality it's the only one of its kind—which is why, when California-based chef Helene Henderson brought her concept to our sandy shores, it was an instant hit.

At Malibu Farm they use mostly whole-wheat flour and whole grains and feature lots of veggies and fruits in the dishes. You'll also find seafood—Henderson grew up fishing. "I love seafood, but let's not deplete our treasures from the sea!" she exclaims. "Our portions are small, and we work hard to offer sustainable seafood only."

Housed in the tony oceanfront Eden Roc Miami Beach, the restaurant has an elevated deck perched perfectly atop the sand dunes of Miami Beach while the indoor dining room is designed to look like a beachy, bohemian cottage with vintage nautical fixtures and black and white photographs.

The avocado pizza (page 128) alone is worth the price of valet parking, as are the grilled octopus and roasted Romanesco and the grass-fed beef burger, topped with Havarti cheese and pepperoncini aioli. Health drives almost the entire menu at this oceanfront oasis. And if you're craving a bit of vice, there's frosé on tap in addition to a full cocktail menu that incorporates infused organic agave syrups and local produce.

FACING Avocado Pizza

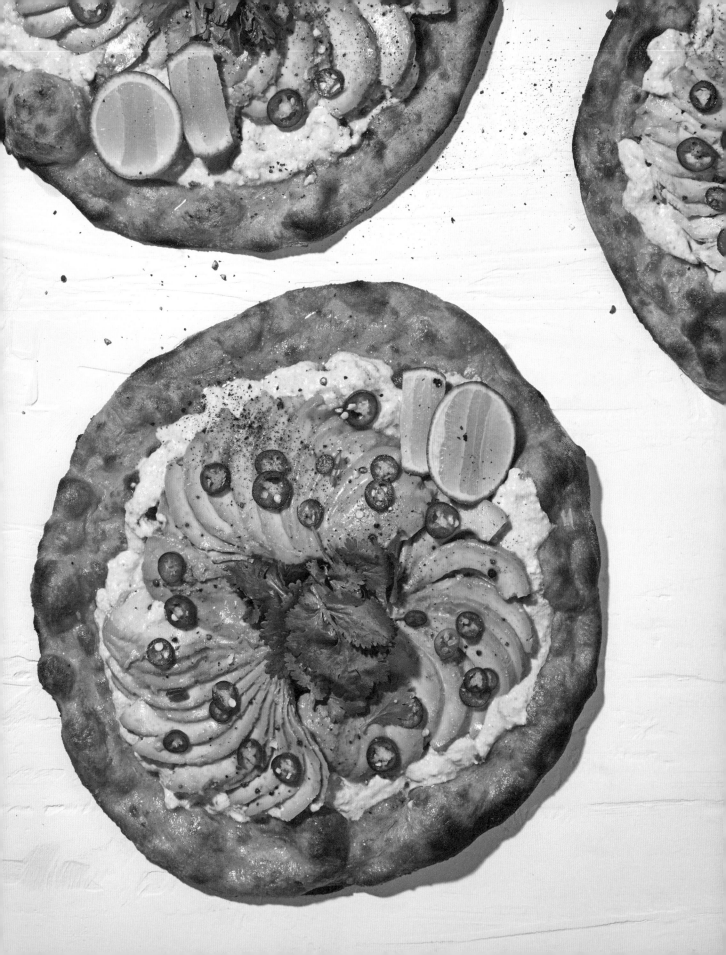

PIZZA DOUGH

4 cups Caputo flour

1 Tbsp Caputo multigrain flour

½ Tbsp salt

1 tsp dry yeast

1 tsp extra-virgin olive oil, plus extra for greasing

1 tsp agave syrup

RICOTTA CREAM

1 jalapeño, chopped

1 serrano chile pepper, seeded and chopped

Grated zest and juice of 1 lemon

¼ cup ricotta

1 Tbsp crème fraîche

Pinch of salt

AGAVE OIL

1 Tbsp agave syrup

1 Tbsp extra-virgin olive oil

Pinch of salt

ASSEMBLY

Pizza Dough (see here)

2 Tbsp Ricotta Cream (see here)

1 avocado, pitted and thinly sliced

Agave Oil (see here), for drizzling

Sea salt and black pepper

½ bunch cilantro

1 serrano pepper, thinly sliced

1 lime, cut in thin wedges

Avocado Pizza

SERVES 2 TO 4 The chef recommends Caputo (or "00") flour for the pizza dough as it is an authentic Italian flour used by *pizzaioli* (pizza makers) to produce a very soft, flavorful thin crust. You can find it at most gourmet markets or online.

PIZZA DOUGH In a mixer fitted with the paddle attachment, combine flours and salt. In another bowl, combine yeast, oil, agave syrup, and ¼ cup water and set aside for 5 minutes. Pour wet ingredients into the flour mixture and knead until a ball of dough forms. Lightly oil a bowl, then add dough and cover with plastic wrap. Set aside to rest for 30 minutes. Form 4 dough balls, place on a tray and cover, and refrigerate for 24 hours.

RICOTTA CREAM In a blender, combine jalapeño, serrano peppers, and lemon juice and blend until smooth.

In a mixing bowl, combine ricotta, crème fraîche, and lemon zest. Add jalapeño mixture and season with salt. Set aside.

AGAVE OIL Combine all ingredients and set aside.

ASSEMBLY Preheat oven to 500°F. Put a round ceramic pizza stone in the oven to warm up.

Take ball of a pizza dough from the refrigerator and bring to room temperature. Stretch dough (using a rolling pin, if needed) as thin as you can without breaking it. Bake for 5 to 10 minutes, until edges are browned and the dough is cooked through.

Top the crust with ricotta cream, spreading it to cover. Arrange avocado on pizza and drizzle agave oil on top. Season with salt and pepper. Top with cilantro, serrano slices, and thinly sliced lime wedges. Serve immediately.

CARAMEL SAUCE

2 cups brown sugar

½ cup corn syrup (optional)

2 cups heavy cream

½ cup (1 stick) butter

CHOCOLATE CAKE

3½ cups all-purpose flour, plus extra for dusting

3½ cups sugar

1 cup unsweetened cocoa powder

1 Tbsp baking soda

1 tsp salt

1½ cups kefir (see Note)

1½ cups canola oil, plus extra for greasing

4 eggs

ASSEMBLY

Confectioners' sugar

Caramel Sauce (see here)

Whipped cream

Maldon sea salt, for finishing

Grilled Chocolate Cake

SERVES 8 It may seem unconventional to grill cake, but trust me on this, you won't regret it. Malibu Farm's delicious chocolate cake is grilled for texture and depth of flavor, then made even more indulgent with a silky caramel sauce. This recipe makes extra caramel sauce, but it lasts for a few weeks in the fridge. When ready to use, simply pop it in the microwave for a few seconds and add it to all your favorite desserts.

CARAMEL SAUCE Combine brown sugar, corn syrup, if using, and 2 Tbsp water in a heavy-bottomed skillet. Cook over low heat for 12 minutes, untouched, until sugar starts to reduce and thicken and large bubbles form.

Meanwhile, combine cream and butter in a saucepan over medium-low heat, until warmed through. Pour this mixture into the skillet and stir until combined. Set aside.

CHOCOLATE CAKE Preheat oven to 375°F. Grease and flour an 8-inch-square cake pan.

In a large bowl, combine flour, sugar, cocoa powder, baking soda, and salt.

In a separate bowl, combine kefir, oil, and eggs. Add wet ingredients to the dry ingredients and stir until well blended.

Pour batter into the prepared cake pan and bake for 30 minutes, or until just firm.

ASSEMBLY Preheat grill to medium-high heat. Dust cake with confectioners' sugar and grill for 2 minutes on each side.

Transfer cake to a serving plate, top with caramel sauce and whipped cream, and finish with salt.

NOTE Kefir is a fermented milk beverage made from kefir grains. Tangy and refreshing, it has the consistency of a drinking-style yogurt and can be found at most supermarkets.

NIKKI BEACH

FRANK FERREIRO
executive chef

Nikki Beach is more than just a restaurant, it's a luxury beach club. Occupying an enviable swath of beachfront land at the southern tip of Miami Beach, this sandy hideaway with those iconic white teepees—which also do double-duty as the brand's logo—has welcomed everyone from celebrities to socialites to curious tourists since it opened back in 1998.

Owners Jack and Lucia Penrod named the beach club after Jack's daughter, Nicole, who passed away when she was only eighteen. The zen-like beachside café that began as a loving tribute has now blossomed into a global empire with thirteen beach clubs and five hotels in far-off locations including Ibiza (Spain), Saint-Tropez (France), and Koh Samui (Thailand). And it's all about the sun-kissed vibes here: buckets of chilled rosé are served at the cabana beds, live DJs provide the perfect soundtrack, and an international menu pays homage to the multiple locations around the world.

Executive Chef Frank Ferreiro has the task of wrangling dishes from the various cuisines to make up the diverse menu, at which he excels. Favorites such as the chilled Andaluz gazpacho, the freshest of sushi boats, and crisp tempura shrimp tacos speak to both the familiarity of classic dishes and the bounty of our coastline, but they also show an international flair that has really helped to define Miami's food culture. And Nikki Beach's legendary Amazing Sundays brunch is not for the faint of heart. We're talking prime rib, whole roasted pork, paella stations, handmade pastas made to order, Nutella waffles, and a resplendent Bloody Mary bar.

One could easily while the day away at this beachy retreat, luxuriating in food and drink while taking in salty ocean breezes, marveling at how magical our city really is—and wondering why we don't do this toes-in-the-sand thing more often.

FACING Sexy Salad and Spaghetti aux Fruits de Mer

SPICY LIME MAYO

⅓ cup mayonnaise

1 Tbsp lime juice

1 tsp chili flakes

1 tsp garlic powder

SEXY SALAD

¼ cup chopped cooked lobster

¼ cup chopped cooked shrimp

¼ cup chopped cooked crabmeat

¼ cup chopped imitation crab

¼ cup chopped avocado

1 Tbsp finely chopped mango

1 Tbsp finely chopped cucumber

2 Tbsp Spicy Lime Mayo (see here)

Sea salt and black pepper

ASSEMBLY

½ cucumber, sliced in rounds

2 lobster claws

Sexy Salad

SERVES 2 This is one of Nikki Beach's most popular dishes, owing to the fact that it goes very well with the lush oceanfront setting. The array of seafood and spicy lime mayo dressing pairs fantastically with chilled rosé, of which there is never a shortage at the al fresco haven.

SPICY LIME MAYO Combine all ingredients in a bowl and mix well until blended.

SEXY SALAD Combine all ingredients in a bowl, seasoning to taste with salt and pepper.

ASSEMBLY Arrange the cucumber in a spiral pattern in the bottom of two bowls. Add salad and garnish with a lobster claw.

¼ cup extra-virgin olive oil

3 cloves garlic, chopped

¼ cup chopped grape
  tomatoes

½ cup white wine

2 Tbsp butter

1 tsp chili flakes

½ cup 16/20 shrimp,
  peeled

¼ lb clams, rinsed and
  scrubbed clean

¼ lb mussels, rinsed and
  scrubbed clean

2 Tbsp lemon juice

1 Tbsp chopped Italian
  parsley

16 oz cooked spaghetti

Arugula, for garnish

Spaghetti aux Fruits de Mer

SERVES 2 Inspired by Nikki Beach's South of France outpost, this tasty dish evokes lazy lunches on the French Riviera. Pair it with a crisp French white wine for a simple and satisfying home meal.

Heat oil in a large skillet over medium-high heat. Add garlic and tomatoes and cook for 3 minutes, until softened. Pour in wine and simmer for 8 to 10 minutes, until the liquid has reduced by half. Stir in butter, chili flakes, shrimp, clams, and mussels and cook for 8 minutes, until mussels and clams have opened. (Discard any unopened shells.) Finish with lemon juice and parsley.

Pour the seafood and sauce over the pasta and toss well. Divide the pasta between two bowls and arrange seafood on top. Garnish with arugula and serve immediately.

OPEN KITCHEN

INES CHATTAS
chef and owner

Every neighborhood should have an Open Kitchen. The multipurpose café serves both coffee and wine and offers family-style take-away dinners and cooking classes in addition to its regular menu. There's a fantastic retail space with gourmet items from artisanal purveyors and hard-to-find European brands. Opened in 2011 by industry veterans Sandra Stefani of Casa Toscana and Ines Chattas of Icebox Café, Open Kitchen was an oasis on the tiny strip in Bay Harbor Islands and quickly garnered a reputation for easy, gourmet meals. Chattas, who is now sole owner and chef, continues to offer comforting yet elevated food.

"We are a neighborhood joint that evolved into much more," says Chattas. "From the food to the service, we aim to create an experience reminiscent of an unforgettable home-cooked meal with friends and family."

A native Argentine, she excels at staples like churrasco steak with chimichurri and homemade empanadas, along with fresh and creative sandwiches and salads like the kale Caesar with pork belly lardons (page 136). "After eight years in Bay Harbor, we have become the neighborhood's kitchen. People working on the island rely on us for a good lunch no matter what budget or palate. We have tons of options," says Chattas.

Stick around long enough and you may find yourself, as I did, with the perfect chicken sandwich in one hand and a glass of bracing iced tea in the other. You might not want to leave, and at Open Kitchen, there's no reason to rush.

FACING Kale Caesar Salad with Crispy Pork Belly Lardons

CRISPY PORK BELLY LARDONS

1 lb pork belly

Salt and black pepper

2 bay leaves

1 star anise

1 Tbsp allspice berries

½ cup white wine

¼ cup apple cider vinegar

1 Tbsp honey

Pinch of brown sugar

CAESAR DRESSING

3 heads garlic, cloves separated and peeled (divided)

2 cups extra-virgin olive oil

3 anchovies

1 egg yolk

¼ cup lemon juice

¼ cup grated Parmesan

½ Tbsp Dijon mustard

1 tsp Worcestershire sauce

Salt and black pepper, to taste

KALE SALAD

1 head kale, stems removed and roughly cut

1 bulb fennel, shaved

¼ red cabbage, shaved

1 cup Caesar Dressing (see here)

Extra-virgin olive oil

½ cup shaved Parmesan

Pork Belly Lardons (see here)

½ cup sourdough croutons

Kale Caesar Salad with Crispy Pork Belly Lardons

SERVES 4 Kale salad is ubiquitous these days but Chef Ines Chattas energizes this dinner table staple with fennel and steps up the indulgence factor with rich pork belly. And her house dressing adds a nice garlicky kick.

CRISPY PORK BELLY LARDONS Preheat oven to 375°F.

Place pork belly in a roasting pan. Season with salt, pepper, bay leaves, star anise, and allspice.

In a separate bowl, combine wine, vinegar, honey, and brown sugar. Pour over pork belly, cover with aluminum foil, and roast for 2 hours, until tender.

Transfer pork belly to a cutting board and set aside to cool. Cut into thin strips.

Heat a large skillet over high heat. Add pork belly slices and fry for 4 to 5 minutes, until crispy. Transfer to a paper towel–lined plate. (Leftover lardons can be stored in an airtight container in the refrigerator for up to seven days.)

CAESAR DRESSING Combine garlic and oil in a small saucepan and cook over low heat for 25 minutes until oil is a caramel color. Set aside to cool. Using a slotted spoon, transfer garlic to a food processor, reserving oil. Add the remaining the ingredients to the food processor and combine. With the motor running, slowly pour in oil and blend until emulsified. Set aside. (Leftover dressing can be stored in the refrigerator for up to five days.)

KALE SALAD Massage kale for 2 to 3 minutes with a splash of oil to soften leaves. In a large bowl, combine kale, fennel, cabbage, and dressing. Add Parmesan, toss, and scatter lardons and croutons on top. Serve.

CARAMELIZED ONIONS

¼ cup extra-virgin olive oil

2 onions, halved lengthwise and thinly sliced

Salt

RISOTTO

¼ cup extra-virgin olive oil

2 shallots, finely chopped

1½ cups arborio rice

½ cup red wine

3 cups beef or vegetable stock

Caramelized Onions (see here)

1 tsp thyme leaves, plus extra for garnish

½ cup grated Gruyère, plus extra for garnish

½ cup grated Parmesan

2 Tbsp butter

Salt and black pepper, to taste

French Onion Risotto

SERVES 2 Onions take center stage in this soothing dish, where you get a bite of beautifully browned, sweet, soft caramelized onions in every comforting spoonful. Gruyère and Parmesan cheese add creaminess and depth.

CARAMELIZED ONIONS Heat oil in a large saucepan over high heat. Add onions and sauté for 1 to 2 minutes, until onions are softened and start to turn translucent. Season with a pinch of salt. Reduce heat to medium-low and cook for another 25 to 30 minutes, stirring occasionally, until caramel-colored. Transfer to a plate and set aside.

RISOTTO Heat oil in the same saucepan over medium heat. Add shallots and cook for 7 to 10 minutes, until lightly golden. Add rice and wine, then reduce heat to low and mix well. Add a ladle of stock and cook until most of the liquid has been absorbed, stirring occasionally.

Add onions and thyme, then continue to add ladles of stock every few minutes, until absorbed, for another 15 minutes. Stir in cheeses and cook for another 3 to 5 minutes, until risotto is al dente and nearly all the stock is absorbed. Remove from heat and stir in butter. Season with salt and pepper.

Divide risotto between two plates. Garnish with Gruyère and thyme. Serve immediately.

PHUC YEA

ANIECE MEINHOLD
co-owner

CESAR ZAPATA
co-owner and chef

Phuc Yea was Miami's first pop-up. Partners Cesar Zapata and Aniece Meinhold had long been perfecting their hospitality chops (he's in the kitchen, she's front of house) and took a chance on a temporary space serving the Vietnamese food of Meinhold's heritage. And despite the less-than-attractive location, adventurous diners flocked downtown for bowls of pho and Vietnamese chicken wings—which provided the impetus for opening multiple permanent spots, including their current Phuc Yea in the MiMo District.

Say the restaurant's name to diners who diligently canvas the city's dining scene, eager not to lose touch with anything noteworthy, and they'll nod approvingly. Oh sure, some of us remember them when they were just starting out as a pop-up downtown. Now they're years into a thriving hospitality business that shows no signs of slowing down.

When Time Out Market launched in South Beach, they looked to the Phuc Yea team to open a counter-service spot serving Vietnamese noodle soup and Pho Mo was born. Now, the food hall location serves an average of thirty gallons of pho a day.

"Cesar and I were kids when we started," says Meinhold. "Now, over fifteen years in, the one thing that keeps us pushing, happy, and coming back for more is nurturing every opportunity to serve and feed the people of our city. As a team, we do not just provide food and drink; we are patrons of hospitality. We have the distinct pleasure of serving all of Miami and creating our version of magic. That is why people keep coming back to us year after year."

FACING Pho Bo and Caramel Chicken Wings

BROTH

2 whole yellow onions, unpeeled

4 (1-inch) pieces ginger, unpeeled

6 lbs beef marrow and neck bones

1 lb beef brisket

7 star anise

6 whole cloves

3 cinnamon sticks (preferably Chinese cinnamon)

1 pod black cardamom

1½ Tbsp salt

1 Tbsp coriander seeds

½ tsp fennel seeds

1 (1-inch) chunk yellow rock sugar (1 oz)

1 cube chicken bouillon

Salt and black pepper, to taste

Pho Bo

SERVES 4 The counter-service spot at Time Out Market in South Beach is where the Phuc Yea team churn out hundreds of bowls of the Vietnamese comfort food also known as pho. The long-simmering broth will fill your kitchen with aromas of star anise, cloves, and ginger, and it's the perfect dish to satisfy and nourish when the temperature drops a bit.

BROTH Place onions and ginger directly over a high-heat flame on a grill or gas stove. Char for 15 minutes, until soften and sweetly fragrant. (You do not have to blacken entire surface, just enough to slightly cook onion and ginger.) Set aside to cool.

Rinse onion under warm running water and remove charred skin. Trim and discard blackened root or stem ends.

If ginger skin is puckered and blistered, smash ginger with the flat side of a knife to loosen the flesh from the skin. Using a sharp paring knife, peel ginger. Rinse ginger under warm running water to wash off blackened bits. Set aside.

Place bones in a large stockpot and cover with cold water. Bring to a boil over high heat and boil for 2 to 3 minutes to release impurities. Drain and rinse bones under warm running water. Scrub stockpot to remove any residue, then return bones to pot.

Add enough water to the pot to cover the bones and bring to a boil over high heat. Reduce heat to medium-low and gently simmer for 10 minutes, skimming off any scum from the surface. Add remaining ingredients and just enough water to cover. Cook, uncovered, for 1½ hours, until brisket is slightly chewy but not tough. Remove the brisket and place in a bowl of cold water for 10 minutes. Drain the meat, cool, then refrigerate. Add one more cup of water and simmer broth for another 1½ hours.

Strain broth through a fine-mesh strainer. If desired, remove any bits of gelatinous tendon from bones to add to your pho bowl. Refrigerate tendon with cooked beef. Discard the rest of the solids.

NOODLES

2 lbs dried or fresh pho
noodles

ASSEMBLY

½ lb raw beef eye of round
or tenderloin, thinly
sliced across the grain
(see Note)

3 scallions, dark green
parts only, cut into thin
rings

1 yellow onion, very thinly
sliced, soaked for
30 minutes in a bowl of
cold water

Bunch of cilantro, coarsely
chopped

Bunch of Thai basil

½ lb beansprouts

1 jalapeño, thinly sliced

4 lime wedges

½ cup hoisin sauce

½ cup Sriracha

Using a ladle, skim off as much fat as possible
from the surface of the broth. Season to taste.

NOODLES If you're using dried noodles, cover
with hot water and soak 15 to 20 minutes, until
softened and opaque white. Drain in colander.
For fresh rice noodles, untangle and place in a
colander, then rinse under cold running water.

Bring a large saucepan of water to a boil. Using
a long-handle strainer, lower noodles into the pan
and blanch for 10 to 20 seconds. Drain noodles,
and transfer to four large individual bowls.
Noodles should fill a third of each bowl.

ASSEMBLY Bring broth to a rolling boil. Place slices
of cooked meat, raw meat, and tendon, if using,
into each noodle bowl. Garnish with scallions,
onion, cilantro, and Thai basil.

Ladle broth into each bowl, distributing hot
liquid evenly so as to slightly cook the raw beef
and warm other ingredients. Serve the pho with
a plate of beansprouts, jalapeño slices, and lime
wedges, with hoisin sauce and Sriracha on the side.

NOTE Try putting the raw beef eye of round or
tenderloin in the freezer for 15 minutes first to make
slicing easier.

CARAMEL SAUCE

2 cups sugar

Juice of ½ lime

1 cup fish sauce

2 small stalks lemongrass, chopped

½ red Thai chile, chopped

1 Tbsp sesame seeds, toasted

½ tsp grated ginger

½ cup sweet chili sauce

CHICKEN WINGS

2 cups canola oil, for frying

2 lbs chicken wings

1 cup Caramel Sauce (see here)

Baby beet greens, for garnish

Caramel Chicken Wings

SERVES 4 These addictive chicken wings are fried "naked," meaning there's no breading to get in the way of the caramel fish sauce that coats them and gives each bite a wondrously umami flavor. Pair them with a delicious Asian beer for a satisfying spin on a game-day staple.

CARAMEL SAUCE In a saucepan, combine sugar, lime juice, and ¼ cup water and cook over medium heat for 5 to 7 minutes, untouched, until caramel color. (To avoid crystallization, do not stir.) Remove from heat and set aside to cool.

Carefully pour in fish sauce and mix gently. Stir in the remaining ingredients and simmer for 10 minutes over low heat. Keep warm.

CHICKEN WINGS Heat oil in a deep fryer or deep saucepan over medium-high heat to 350°F. Working in batches, add wings to the oil and deep-fry for 6 to 8 minutes, turning occasionally, until evenly deep golden brown and completely cooked through. Transfer wings to a paper towel–lined plate to drain.

Heat caramel sauce mixture in a nonstick wok or saucepan over high heat and bring it to a boil. Cook for 45 seconds, or until mixture has reduced by half. Toss wings in the sauce.

Transfer the wings to a serving plate and garnish with baby beet greens.

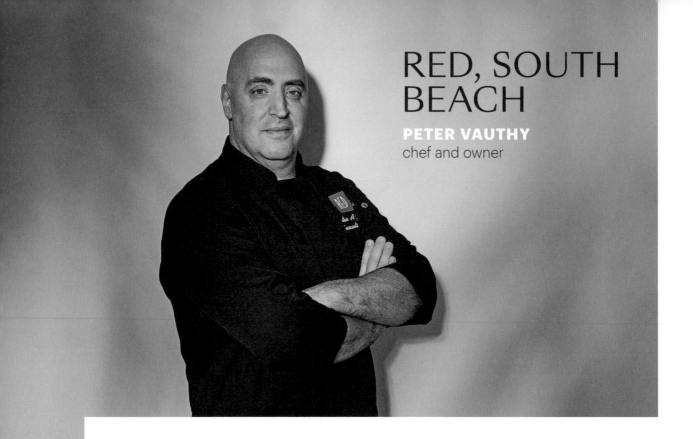

RED, SOUTH BEACH

PETER VAUTHY
chef and owner

Back in 2008, when Chef Peter Vauthy opened Red, the Steakhouse, beef houses were cropping up in the Miami dining scene almost monthly. Some of those steakhouses eventually shuttered, casualties of Miami's competitive and fickle market, yet Red has thrived, serving its signature steaks and superb cocktails to a steady throng of locals and out-of-towners.

"Relationships are the key to success," explains Vauthy. His first-hand suppliers offer him dibs on their freshest catch or latest batch. From fisheries to local farms, personal contacts ring Vauthy first when new ingredients become available. "My rolodex is my arsenal," he quips.

This "phone-to-table" approach results in daily specials such as fresh Alaskan King Crab flown in straight from the Bering Sea, scarce finds including spiny Brittany blue lobster, and batches of porcini mushrooms

the size of hands. Vauthy is also committed to serving only Certified Angus Beef Prime, with a mammoth porterhouse and a petite filet mignon as stars of the show. The steaks arrive at the table well-marbled, expertly seared, judiciously seasoned, and delightfully tender. Also impressive are seafood dishes like the mussels Diavolo, the tuna poke, and the creamy lobster mac 'n' cheese.

Vauthy is a bit of a social media guru, keeping his Instagram and Twitter armed full of hunger-inducing shots and delivering an insider's look at his creations and kitchen. Happily for us, the subjects of those photos are even more impressive and delicious in person.

8 ears Florida sweet corn

2 Tbsp butter (divided)

3 cloves garlic, thinly
sliced

1 Tbsp sliced shallot

2 cups heavy cream

1 Tbsp chopped Italian
parsley

1 Tbsp chopped chives

Salt and black pepper

1 cup breadcrumbs

Sweet Creamed Corn

SERVES 4 This is one of the most popular side dishes at Red and goes wonderfully with the hearty steak on page 146. Simmering the freshly shucked corn cobs in cream infuses the dish with a depth of flavor, and the chives and shallots give it a gourmet touch.

Shave corn kernels off of the cobs and set aside. Reserve the cobs.

Melt 1 tablespoon butter in a large saucepan over medium heat. Add garlic and shallot and sauté for 4 minutes, until softened. Add the reserved corn cobs and cream and simmer for 20 minutes, until reduced by half. Remove corn cobs and discard.

Preheat oven to 400°F.

Melt the remaining tablespoon of butter in a skillet over medium heat. Add corn kernels, parsley, and chives and sauté for 3 to 5 minutes, until tender. Stir in ½ cup corn-infused cream and mix until evenly combined, adding more cream if desired. Season with salt and pepper.

Place mixture in a baking dish, top with the breadcrumbs, and bake for 10 to 12 minutes until crumbs are golden brown. Serve hot.

CRAB CRUST

1 cup mayonnaise

1 cup panko breadcrumbs

1 Tbsp Dijon mustard

1 Tbsp chopped red bell pepper

1 Tbsp finely chopped Italian parsley

3 cloves garlic, finely chopped

½ lb lump crabmeat

STEAK

1 (16-oz) Certified Angus Beef Prime rib eye

1 Tbsp salt

Black pepper

Crab Crust (see here)

Sweet Creamed Corn (page 145), to serve

Crab-Crusted Rib-Eye Steak

SERVES 2 TO 4 A scoop of creamy crab on top of a sizzling steak takes surf and turf to a whole new level. This is Chef Vauthy's play on Steak Oscar, a classic dish that was a favorite of Sweden's King Oscar. But you don't have to be royalty to appreciate its decadence.

CRAB CRUST In a large bowl, combine mayonnaise, panko, mustard, bell pepper, parsley, and garlic. Fold in crabmeat and mix thoroughly. Set aside.

STEAK Preheat oven to 400°F.

Season steak on both sides with salt and pepper. In a cast-iron skillet set over high heat, sear steak for 2 to 3 minutes until a golden brown crust forms. Flip over and place pan into the oven. Cook for 4 to 6 minutes, or until the steak reaches an internal temperature of 135°F for medium-rare. Remove from oven.

Cover the steak with a ½-inch layer of crab crust and roast for another 5 to 7 minutes, or until the crust is golden brown and hot. Divide the steak among four individual plates and serve with the creamed corn.

SALUMERIA 104/ SPRIS

ANGELO MASARIN
chef and co-owner, Salumeria 104

Part trattoria, part cured meats and cheese shop, Salumeria 104 is an Italian food lover's dream. Whether it is a charcuterie board piled high with thinly sliced meats, crusty bread, and briny olives or a steaming bowl of home-made cavatelli in a luscious tomato sauce, the dining experience is sublime at this cheerful spot where the waiters—and most of the clientele—banter in Italian. Of course, much of that is owing to Chef Angelo Masarin's hospitality and love of pristine ingredients. Originally from Treviso, Italy, Masarin arrived in Miami in 2009 and honed his culinary skills at Sardinia Enoteca Ristorante (page 152) and Casa Tua before partnering with Graspa Group restaurateurs Graziano Sbroggio and Carlo Donadoni to open this restaurant-shop hybrid. He now helms two locations—the original in midtown Miami and a sibling in Coral Gables— and both serve the kind of rustic, belly-filling Italian dishes that are a hit in their respective neighborhoods.

Spris Lincoln Road, another of their restaurants, has served thin-crusted wood-burning brick-oven pizzas and specialty sandwiches and salads to hungry shoppers and strollers for more than two decades. The lure is easy: if you love people-watching it tends to be Miami's best spot. The outdoor café setting attracts tourists, locals, pet lovers, and many interesting personalities, but the laid-back atmosphere, efficient service, and wonderful food really bring the crowds back for more. Chef Carlo Donadoni is the creative mind behind the menu here as well as at Spuntino Bakery and Catering. Even as Lincoln Road evolves and some of our beloved home-grown concepts shutter, Spris continues to thrive. And we look forward to many more afternoons spent grazing on pesto-topped pizza while taking in the scene on the famous pedestrian mall.

FACING Tiramisu

PIZZA DOUGH

2⅓ cups strong bread flour (300 g), plus extra for dusting

1 tsp instant yeast

1 tsp salt

1 Tbsp extra-virgin olive oil

SAUCE

½ cup passata

Handful of basil, chopped

Salt, to taste

ASSEMBLY

Strong bread flour, for dusting

Pizza Dough (see here)

Sauce (see here)

4½ oz fresh mozzarella, sliced

10 cherry tomatoes, halved

Extra-virgin olive oil, for drizzling

Salt and pepper, to taste

2¼ oz local burrata

¼ cup basil leaves

4 oz sliced mortadella with pistachio

Pizza Mortazza

SERVES 4 This is the authentic Roman title for a rustic pizza loaded with wafer-thin slices of pistachio-laden mortadella, indulgent burrata, and creamy mozzarella. It makes for a deliciously savory brunch dish or light main course. For the pizza dough, Chef Carlo Donadoni uses a strong bread flour, which has more protein than standard all-purpose flour, creates more gluten, and ultimately gives it that desirable chew factor.

PIZZA DOUGH Put flour in a large bowl, then stir in yeast and salt. Make a well and pour in ¾ cup warm water and the oil. Using a wooden spoon, bring in flour and mix until you have a soft, wet dough. Transfer dough to a lightly floured surface and knead for 5 minutes until smooth. Cover with a dish towel and set aside for 20 to 30 minutes. (You can leave the dough to rise if desired, but it's not essential for a thin crust.)

SAUCE In a large bowl, combine passata and basil. Season with salt to taste. Set aside.

ASSEMBLY Preheat oven to 450°F. Lightly flour two large baking sheets.

If you've let the dough rise, give it a quick knead. Divide dough into 2 balls.

Using a rolling pin, roll out a dough ball on a lightly floured surface to a diameter of 10 inches. (The dough needs to be really thin as it will rise when it bakes.) Repeat. Transfer the discs onto the prepared baking sheets.

Ladle sauce over the pizza bases and smooth out with the back of the spoon. Scatter mozzarella and tomatoes on top, then drizzle with oil and season with salt and pepper. Bake the pizzas for 8 to 10 minutes, until crisp.

Dot the pizzas with burrata and basil, then drizzle with a little more olive oil. Add mortadella and slice. Serve immediately.

6 egg yolks

½ cup sugar

3 cups heavy cream

2 cups mascarpone

2 cups brewed espresso

1 Tbsp Kahlúa liqueur

1 Tbsp Frangelico liqueur

2½ (7-oz) bags Vicenzovo ladyfingers

Unsweetened cocoa powder, for garnish

Tiramisu

SERVES 8 TO 10 Tiramisu is one of the most revered and widely known desserts, and Salumeria's version has all the makings of a classic. It is deceptively easy to make, requires very little effort, and always makes an impression. Simply prepare it a day in advance and when it comes to serving, sprinkle cocoa powder on top. Many of the ingredients can be purchased at Salumeria's market, as well.

In the bowl of a stand mixer fitted with the whisk attachment, combine egg yolks and sugar on high speed for 3 minutes, or until the sugar is dissolved and the yolks are stiff.

In a separate bowl, whip cream until firm. Fold in mascarpone, then fold mixture into the egg yolks.

In a separate bowl, combine espresso, Kahlúa, and Frangelico. Spread a thin layer of the mascarpone mousse in the bottom of an 8- × 8-inch dish. Quickly dip a ladyfinger in the espresso mixture and place in the dish. Repeat with ladyfingers until the entire surface is covered. Spread half of the remaining mascarpone mousse overtop. Repeat the process with the remaining ladyfingers and mousse. Square the sides and smooth the top. Cover and refrigerate overnight.

Sprinkle cocoa powder all over the top to finish, then serve.

SARDINIA
ENOTECA
RISTORANTE

TONY GALLO
restaurateur and co-owner

PIETRO VARDEU
chef and co-owner

Look around Sunset Harbor today and it's hard to imagine a time when its streets weren't jam-packed with boutiques, fancy juice bars, and fitness studios jostling for position. But the area was far from glamorous when Sardinia's co-owners, restaurateur Tony Gallo and chef Pietro Vardeu, decided to take a chance back in 2006 and create their version of the perfect Italian neighborhood restaurant—before there was much of a "neighborhood" to speak of. It worked. More than a decade later, Sardinia has much more competition in the area but still reigns supreme as a favored local destination for marvelous food and a stellar wine list.

"Sardinia is not your typical Italian-American restaurant," says Gallo. "We make our own mozzarella and burrata cheeses and cook our meats and fish in a wood-burning oven."

And seafood, of course, plays a big role in a regional cuisine that captures Italy's coastal bounty. Favorites include dishes of steamed mussels with fava beans, the signature spaghetti topped with shaved *bottarga di muggine* (page 154), and branzino baked in salt crust. Plus antipasti platters piled high with pecorino and salumi, gnocchi made in-house with lamb sugo, and of course fregola, those tiny pearls of pasta similar to nutty couscous—they all have a home here.

If the atmosphere inside Sardinia didn't already transport you to the Italian island, the ultra-professional front of house team most certainly will. Unlike some restaurants that push you through a meal, Sardinia's team is excited to show you what their kitchen cohorts are cooking up and don't mind if you spend all night.

FREGOLA

½ cup fregola

2 Tbsp extra-virgin olive oil

1 large carrot, chopped (1 cup)

1 large stalk celery, chopped (1 cup)

CLAMS

¼ cup extra-virgin olive oil

2 cloves garlic, finely chopped

2 Tbsp dried rosemary

2 Tbsp dried thyme

1 tsp chili flakes

Pinch of saffron

4 cups white wine

24 fresh littleneck clams, rinsed and scrubbed clean

Fregola (see here)

24 cherry tomatoes, halved

Salt and black pepper, to taste

Fregoletta

SERVES 4 This classic and sophisticated Sardinian dish is easy to prepare when you're short on time. Fregola, a small pasta similar to Israeli couscous, is simmered in a tasty broth made rich with clams, tomatoes, and saffron. Fregola can be found in Italian specialty markets or online.

FREGOLA In a small saucepan, combine fregola and 1 cup water and bring to a boil over high heat. Reduce heat to medium and boil gently for 6 minutes, until just cooked. Drain and set aside.

Heat oil in a large skillet over medium heat. Add carrot and celery and sauté for 7 to 10 minutes, until tender. Add fregola and cook for another 5 minutes. Set aside.

CLAMS Heat oil in a large saucepan over medium heat. Add garlic, herbs, chili flakes, and saffron and sauté for 30 seconds, until fragrant. Pour in wine and bring to a boil. Reduce heat to medium-low and simmer for 3 minutes, until reduced by half. Add clams, cover, and cook for 6 to 8 minutes, transferring clams to a bowl as they open. (Discard any unopened clams.)

Add the fregola mixture and tomatoes and cook for another 2 minutes, until fregola is tender and sauce is slightly thickened. Add clams, season with salt and pepper, and cook until warmed through. Serve immediately.

½ cup extra-virgin olive oil

12 cherry tomatoes, halved

2 cloves garlic, thinly sliced

1 Tbsp chili flakes

1 lb spaghetti

½ cup finely chopped Italian parsley (optional)

½ cup mullet bottarga

Grated zest of 2 lemons

Spaghetti Bottarga

SERVES 4 Bottarga, a specialty of southern Italy, is the roe of gray mullet that has been salted, pressed, and air-dried. It adds a lovely briny flavor and nuttiness to this popular Sardinian pasta dish. The addition of cherry tomatoes lends a complementary slightly sweet note.

Bring a large pot of water to a boil.

Heat oil in a large skillet over medium-low heat. Add tomatoes, garlic, and chili flakes and cook for 2 minutes, until fragrant. Remove from heat.

Add spaghetti to the pot of boiling water and cook according to package directions, until just al dente. Drain, reserving 1 cup pasta liquid, then add spaghetti to the skillet. Stir in parsley, if using, and toss over medium heat. Add a little reserved liquid if needed.

Transfer pasta to a serving platter or individual shallow bowls. Garnish with shaved bottarga and lemon zest and serve immediately.

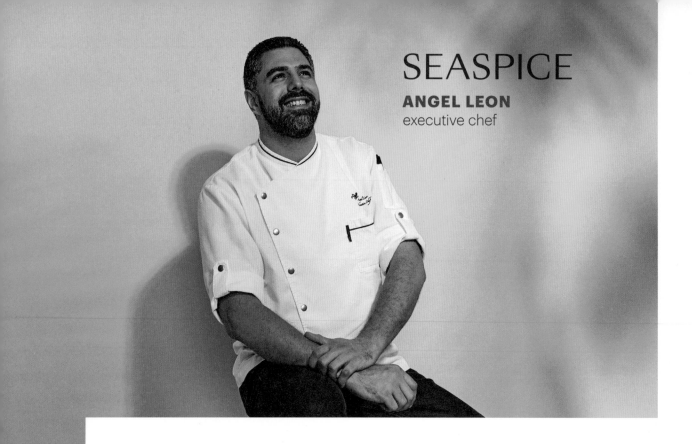

SEASPICE

ANGEL LEON
executive chef

On any given day Seaspice offers a visual smorgasbord, though sometimes it can verge on overstimulation. The million-dollar yachts pulling up to the picturesque dock, the outdoor patio filled with beautiful people dancing to live DJ music, a parade of servers holding magnums of champagne festooned with sparklers. And over there, a table of *Real Housewives* gossiping and preening for cellphone photos. But then the food hits the table and suddenly everyone is paying attention. The fish in the wood-fired casserole spiked with salsa verde (page 158) is excellent and superbly cooked. More than that, the transportive dish takes us on an exhilarating voyage around the world, through culinary traditions as disparate as Italian and Indian. And for one blessed moment, it's the only thing.

In 2014 the Miami River wasn't glamorous, nor did it have a nightlife option. But when restaurateurs Carlos and Maryam Miranda opened this waterfront spot, they helped to regenerate the once-industrial stretch of waterfront and paved the way for more upscale projects to succeed there as well. The former seaplane hangar, with large warehouse-like windows and a striking "chandelier" by artist Carlos Betancourt, is plenty swanky, but it's the culinary team, led by Executive Chef Angel Leon, that makes every visit to Seaspice memorable.

From the seafood towers and the excellent puffed pita that starts every meal to the made-from-scratch pastas and wood-oven-fired casseroles of fresh fish, Seaspice is both accessible and elevated, straddling both the city and sea—and somehow manages to do it all with class.

CITRIC SALSA VERDE

2 cups chopped cilantro

2 cups chopped Italian parsley

2 cloves garlic

1 (½-inch) piece ginger, peeled

Juice of 10 lemons (2 cups)

½ cup extra-virgin olive oil

FISH

2 lbs local yellowtail, deboned, butterflied open, and tail intact (ask your fishmonger)

Salt and black pepper

GRILLED VEGETABLES

6 to 8 sugar snap peas

6 cherry tomatoes, halved

2 Tbsp extra-virgin olive oil

Salt and black pepper

CASSEROLE BASE

1 Tbsp extra-virgin olive oil

1 small clove garlic, sliced

½ Tbsp sliced shallot

2 Tbsp white wine

1½ cups fish stock

1 Tbsp Citric Salsa Verde (see here)

Salt and black pepper

1 tsp butter

Pinch of chopped Italian parsley, plus more for garnish

Market Fish Casserole

SERVES 2 TO 4 This showstopper of a dish is presented with bright and citrusy salsa verde. It's the type of dish you prepare when you want to impress the most discerning of guests.

CITRIC SALSA VERDE Place all ingredients in a blender and blend until smooth. Set aside. (Leftover salsa verde will keep in the refrigerator for five to seven days.)

FISH Build a medium-hot fire in a charcoal grill or preheat a gas grill to medium-high heat. Score the skin of the fish by cutting slashes into it lengthwise, then crosswise. Season with salt and pepper.

Place fish on the hot grill, skin side down, and grill for 8 minutes, until nearly cooked through. Set aside.

GRILLED VEGETABLES Preheat grill to low heat. Toss vegetables, oil, salt, and pepper together in a bowl. Add vegetables to the grill (using a grill mat if needed) and grill gently for 1 to 2 minutes per side. Remove from grill and set aside.

CASSEROLE BASE Heat oil in a skillet over medium heat. Add garlic and shallot and sauté for 4 minutes, until fragrant but not brown. Deglaze with wine.

Add stock and citric salsa verde and season with salt and pepper. Simmer for 5 minutes on low heat. Finish with butter and parsley. Remove from the heat.

ASSEMBLY Preheat oven to 350°F.

Place fish in a casserole dish, pour in the casserole base and top with 1 cup citric salsa verde (or enough to cover), then arrange the vegetables around the fish. Bake for 10 to 12 minutes, then garnish with parsley and serve.

LEMON MOUSSE

3 sheets gelatin

Grated zest and juice of
2 lemons

½ cup sugar

3 eggs, separated

¾ cup heavy cream

ASSEMBLY

Whipped cream

Raspberries

Lemon curd (optional)

Lemon Mousse

SERVES 3 TO 4 This wonderfully tart mousse is the perfect way to end a meal of fresh seafood. The lemon flavor cleanses the palate while the silky creaminess is pure indulgence. Be sure to make this dessert a day in advance as it requires overnight chilling time.

LEMON MOUSSE Soak the gelatin sheets in water until they bloom.

Place the bloomed gelatin sheets and lemon juice in a saucepan and heat over low heat.

In the bowl of an electric mixer, combine sugar and lemon zest. Add egg yolks and whip until mixture has doubled in volume and is lighter in color. Slowly add the gelatin mixture to the bowl.

Place the bowl in a large bowl of ice water and stir mixture frequently, until thickened. Refrigerate for 15 minutes, until fluffy but not stiff.

In a separate bowl, whip egg whites until medium peaks form.

In another bowl, whip heavy cream to soft peaks.

Slowly fold in the egg whites into the lemon mixture. Fold in whipped cream. Immediately pipe mousse into dessert glasses, cover, and refrigerate overnight.

ASSEMBLY Garnish mousse with whipped cream, berries, and lemon curd, if using, and serve.

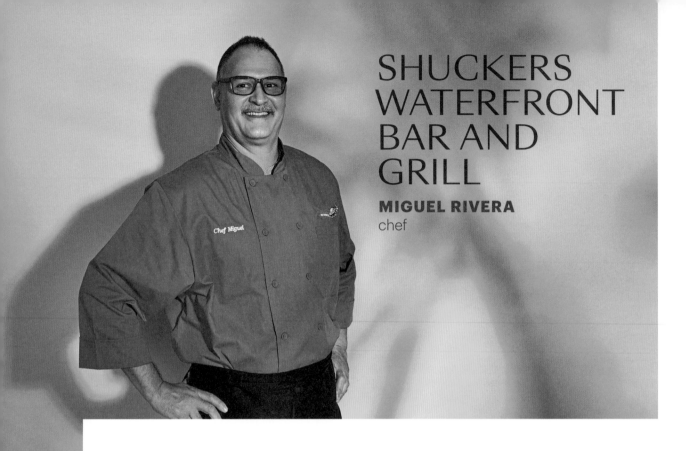

SHUCKERS WATERFRONT BAR AND GRILL

MIGUEL RIVERA
chef

In a city that often rewards flash and glitz over the humble and simple, Shuckers stands tall as the real deal. Part sports bar, part boater's hideaway, Shuckers is situated on a small island in the middle of Biscayne Bay between mainland Miami and Miami Beach. Boaters can dock their vessels on one of the multiple docks, which makes this establishment a popular pit stop for nautical enthusiasts seeking fresh eats and cold drinks.

Their happy hour is legendary among locals, who flock to their world-class raw bar. On game days, the bar is packed with people elbowing for viewing space near the more than thirty flat-screen TVs. And every self-respecting Miamian knows that Shuckers is the place to order classics such as wings, ribs, and fish dip—all of which are equally fresh and satisfying. The rest of the crowd-pleasing menu is laced with fan faves including burgers and fries, juicy fried fish fillets, and peel-and-eat shrimp.

For a city that is surrounded by water, Miami is painfully short on waterfront restaurants, and Shuckers has become the natural choice for those looking to soak in salty Florida vibes. It's a place where you could easily while away the day, chatting over garlic shrimp (page 165) and well-priced pitchers of beer and taking in legendary Miami sunsets over the water. It's why Shuckers has been in business for over twenty-five years and why we look forward to returning there time and again.

¼ cup extra-virgin olive oil

¼ cup (½ stick) butter (divided)

5 cloves garlic, finely chopped

½ cup + 2 Tbsp white wine

Salt and black pepper

7 oz Spanish chorizo, cut diagonally

1 lb Chilean mussels, rinsed and scrubbed clean

½ bulb fennel, grilled and chopped

½ small leek, white and light green parts only, cut in small to medium dice

4 grape tomatoes, halved

Bread of choice, to serve

Chilean Mussels

SERVES 4 When you're looking for an easy, full-flavored meal but pressed for time, Chef Miguel Rivera's Chilean mussels recipe checks all the boxes. Plump mussels are steamed to perfection and served with crusty bread to mop up all that savory, full-bodied chorizo-wine sauce.

Heat oil and 2 tablespoons butter in a skillet over medium-low heat. Add garlic and sauté for 1 to 2 minutes, until garlic is fragrant and lightly golden. Pour in wine and cook for another 10 minutes, until reduced by half. Season with salt and pepper.

Add chorizo and cook for 30 seconds. Add mussels, cover, and simmer for 4 to 6 minutes, until mussels have opened. Stir in fennel, leek, tomatoes, and the remaining 2 tablespoons of butter. Season with salt and pepper to taste. Discard any unopened shells.

Transfer to a serving bowl and serve with bread of your choice.

SAUCE

1 Tbsp butter

5 cloves garlic, finely chopped

2 Tbsp finely chopped shallots

½ cup white wine

1 tsp seafood base or clam juice

¼ cup cornstarch

Salt and black pepper

GARLIC SHRIMP

1 Tbsp butter

3 cloves garlic, finely chopped

1 lb 16/20 shrimp, peeled and deveined, with tails intact

12 grape tomatoes, halved

¼ cup white wine

Sauce (see here)

2 Tbsp chopped parsley, for garnish

½ lemon, in wedges, to serve

Bread of choice, to serve

Garlic Shrimp

SERVES 4 Shuckers is known for great seafood dishes that are equally delicious and unfussy and this one hits all the right notes. The garlic and white wine sauce complements the sweet shrimp beautifully. Pair it with a nice leafy salad and a chilled white wine for a light meal.

SAUCE Melt butter in a skillet over medium heat. Add garlic and shallots and sauté for 4 minutes, until softened and fragrant. Add wine and seafood base (or clam juice) and bring to a boil. Cook for 8 minutes, until liquid has reduced by half. Pour in ¾ cup water and mix.

In a bowl, combine cornstarch and ¼ cup water. Slowly pour a little of the mixture into the skillet (you may not need all of it) and cook for 5 minutes, until sauce has thickened. Season to taste with salt and pepper.

GARLIC SHRIMP Heat butter in a large skillet over medium-high heat. Add garlic and cook for a minute, until fragrant. Add shrimp, tomatoes, and wine and sauté for 1 minute.

Pour in sauce and simmer for 2 to 3 minutes, until shrimp are fully cooked. Transfer to a serving bowl, garnish with parsley, and serve with lemon wedges and bread.

SOTTOSALE/ ESOTICO

DANIELE DALLA POLA
mixologist at Esotico

IVO MAZZON
chef at Sottosale

Chef Ivo (Giovanni) Mazzon was born and raised in Treviso, Italy, and has always had a passion for the good things in life. After graduating from culinary school in Italy in the late nineties, he moved to America and worked his way up to becoming an executive member at Graspa Group in January of 2017. "I left Italy to experience life out of my comfort zone," explains Mazzon.

At Sottosale, an Italian home-style restaurant, it is Mazzon's warm hospitality that'll make you feel right at home, and his own modern spin on elevated Italian classics that'll keep you satiated and satisfied. Pasta and pizza are obviously the stars on the menu but light bites like the carne salata with arugula (page 168) are presented with such a deft and beautiful touch as to make us whip out our camera for the perfect shot—and then devour them immediately.

And when it comes to cocktails, not many can top Daniele Dalla Pola. Dalla Pola has been a longtime fixture in South Beach, having opened the famous Segafredo L'Originale on Lincoln Road twenty years ago with Graspa Group founder Graziano Sbroggio, before opening his chic ode to tiki, Esotico, in 2019. Not only is he a sophisticated connoisseur of exotic drinks and one of the world's top tropical barkeeps, he also happens to be an expert on authentic tiki culture, having immersed himself in the lifestyle for decades. "A lifetime in the making, Esotico Miami is my dream come true," says Dalla Pola. "I'm proud to bring my expertise and experience to one of the most beautiful and adventurous cities on the planet."

ORGEAT SYRUP

1¾ cups almond paste
(marzipan)

2½ cups simple syrup

2 tsp orange blossom
water or rosewater

DAN'S #9

3½ cups Orgeat Syrup
(see here)

3½ oz ginger juice

3½ oz Alamea spiced rum

COCKTAIL

1 oz Dan's #9
(see here)

½ oz lime juice

½ oz Bacardi Añejo
Cuatro rum

1½ oz Alamea spiced rum

2 dashes Alamea
pimento rum liqueur

2 dashes Angostura bitters

Crushed ice

Mint sprig, for garnish

Esotico Rum Cup

SERVES 1 *Okole maluna*, Miami! Made with a blend of rums, fresh lime juice, and a spiced almond syrup, this cocktail will take your palate on a voyage to the tropics. Your greatest challenge will be having just the one.

ORGEAT SYRUP Combine all ingredients in a blender. Transfer to a bottle or an airtight container and set aside. Makes 1 quart. (Leftover syrup can be stored in the fridge for up to ten days.)

DAN'S #9 Combine all ingredients in a blender. Transfer to a bottle or an airtight container and set aside. Makes 1 quart. (Leftover syrup can be stored in the fridge for up to ten days.)

COCKTAIL Combine all ingredients except mint and pour unstrained into a double old-fashioned glass or a Kahiko mai tai glass. Garnish with mint sprig.

16 oz high-grade beef
  striploin, trimmed of fat

1 tsp black pepper

3 cups salt

¼ cup extra-virgin olive oil

2 Tbsp lemon juice

2 Tbsp sour orange juice

2 cups arugula

Warm ciabatta, to serve

Lemon wedges, to serve

Carne Salata e Rucola

SERVES 2 Carne salata is an Italian delicacy originating in the town of Tenno. Lean, high-quality beef is cured in salt for days and then served raw and thinly sliced as carpaccio, as we see here. Chef Ivo Mazzon recommends enjoying this tasty dish with hot crunchy ciabatta and a nice glass of Italian red wine, or a dry and mineral-rich white.

Massage beef for 3 to 4 minutes. Season with pepper. Roll beef in salt, then place on a baking sheet and cover with the remaining salt. Place a heavy pan on top of the meat and refrigerate for 36 to 48 hours.

In a bowl, combine oil and citrus juices and whisk together.

Using a brush, remove salt from meat. Thinly slice the beef and arrange on a serving platter, then top with arugula and drizzle sauce over top. Serve with warm ciabatta and lemon wedges.

VILLA AZUR

CARLOS TORRES
chef

Villa Azur came about when three friends—Jean-Philippe Bernard, Michael Martin, and Paul Breuza—set out to combine their shared love of French glamor, Mediterranean cuisine, and flawless service. The result is this stunner of a restaurant, reminiscent of a French villa and complete with an elegant sitting room outfitted in linen drapes, bookshelves stocked with photography tomes, and a romantic fireplace. A long bar sparkles with candlelight. The enchanted open-air courtyard is finished with plush tufted white leather couches and surrounded by tropical flora. The overall feeling is nothing short of luxurious.

It's the kind of Miami spot that attracts jet-setters and the well-heeled set but also welcomes locals looking for a glam night out. The restaurant's Thursday night dinner parties are legendary, with sparkler-festooned champagne bottles paraded through the dining room, live DJs holding court, and hours-long festivities that go well into the early morning hours.

And lucky for us the food lives up to the magical décor, courtesy of Chef Carlos Torres's menu of seafood and grilled steaks. A full raw bar's worth of sea-culled delicacies are proffered—oysters, clams, langoustines, lobster, and Petrossian caviar—in all their glorious forms. But despite the restaurant's Côte d'Azur leanings, there's plenty to keep it contemporary and creative. Their cauliflower cakes (page 171) are a plant-based play on the crab-filled classics but lighter and more suited to veggie-forward diners, while the scallop dish (page 172) will have you sopping up every bit of its silky parsnip purée. That mix of bacchanalia and technique keeps things exciting and ensures guests keep an eye out for what Villa Azur will do next.

AJO BLANCO

1 clove garlic

1 Tbsp finely chopped ginger

1 Tbsp almond flour

1 (13½-oz) can coconut milk

1 tsp sherry vinegar

AVOCADO REMOULADE

1 avocado

1 tsp ketchup

1 tsp Dijon mustard

1 tsp Worcestershire sauce

1 tsp Tabasco sauce

1 tsp chopped scallion

1 tsp chopped shallot

1 tsp capers

1 tsp chopped fennel fronds

1 tsp chopped Italian parsley

CAULIFLOWER

1 (1-lb) head cauliflower

½ shallot, finely chopped

1 tsp chopped Italian parsley

1 tsp chopped tarragon

1 tsp chopped cilantro

Grated zest of 1 lemon

1 cup Ajo Blanco (see here)

Salt and black pepper, to taste

ASSEMBLY

2 Tbsp coconut oil

2 cups Cauliflower (see here)

1 lb kataifi dough (see Note)

½ cup Avocado Remoulade (see here)

3 cups mixed salad greens

½ Tbsp lemon juice

1½ Tbsp extra-virgin olive oil

Salt and black pepper, to taste

Cauliflower Cakes

SERVES 2 A vegan spin on the classic crab cake, this version uses meaty roasted cauliflower to delicious effect.

AJO BLANCO Place all ingredients in a blender and process until smooth.

AVOCADO REMOULADE In a bowl, combine avocado, ketchup, Dijon, Worcestershire, and Tabasco and mash with a fork until smooth. Add the remaining ingredients and mix well.

CAULIFLOWER Preheat oven to 350°F.

Place whole cauliflower on a baking sheet and roast for 20 minutes, until tender. Remove from oven and chop into small, bite-sized florets. Transfer florets to a large bowl, add shallot, herbs, lemon zest, and ajo blanco, and mix well. Season with salt and pepper.

ASSEMBLY Preheat oven to 350°F.

Heat coconut oil in an ovenproof skillet over medium-high heat. Form the cauliflower mixture into four 3-inch patties, about 1 inch thick. Wrap cauliflower cakes in kataifi dough to hold them together and create a crispy breading.

Carefully add cakes to pan and sear for 3 minutes on each side, until golden brown. Place pan in oven and bake for 7 minutes, until cooked through.

Spoon the avocado remoulade into the center of two plates. Arrange the cauliflower cakes on top.

In a bowl, combine salad greens, lemon juice, oil, salt and pepper. Add salad to each plate and serve immediately.

NOTE Kataifi is a shredded phyllo pastry often used in buttery and syrupy Lebanese pastries. It can be found in specialty supermarkets.

PARSNIP PURÉE

4 parsnips, peeled and cut into 1-inch pieces (1 lb)

4 cups milk

BRAISED RADISHES

3 breakfast radishes, halved lengthwise

¼ cup (½ stick) butter

PAN-ROASTED SCALLOPS

1 lb (U-10) scallops

Salt and white pepper

2 Tbsp vegetable oil

ASSEMBLY

Salmon roe, for garnish (optional)

Pea tendrils, for garnish

Pan-Roasted Scallops with Parsnip Purée and Braised Radishes

SERVES 2 The mildly sweet flavor of the scallops and the caramelized crust they get when seared in a super-hot pan make this dish swoon-worthy. And the parsnip purée adds a creamy, decadent note to the dish.

PARSNIP PURÉE Place parsnips and milk in a large saucepan set over medium heat and cook for 20 minutes, or until parsnips are tender. Transfer mixture to a blender and purée. Keep warm.

BRAISED RADISHES Place radishes and butter in a small saucepan set over low heat and cook for 20 minutes, or until radishes are translucent. Drain butter, then set radishes aside.

PAN-ROASTED SCALLOPS Season scallops with salt and pepper.

Heat oil in a small skillet over high heat. Add scallops, flat-side down, and sear, untouched, for 1½ to 2 minutes, until browned. Flip scallops and sear for another 1 to 2 minutes, until opaque. Transfer to a plate and serve immediately.

ASSEMBLY Pour parsnip purée onto a serving plate, then arrange scallops on top. Garnish with radishes, salmon roe, if using, and pea tendrils. Serve immediately.

Metric Conversion Chart

Volume			Weight			Linear		
Imperial	**Metric**		**Imperial**	**Metric**		**Imperial**	**Metric**	
⅛ tsp	0.5 mL		½ oz	15 g		⅛ inch	3 mm	
¼ tsp	1 mL		1 oz	30 g		¼ inch	6 mm	
½ tsp	2.5 mL		2 oz	60 g		½ inch	12 mm	
¾ tsp	4 mL		3 oz	85 g		¾ inch	2 cm	
1 tsp	5 mL		4 oz (¼ lb)	115 g		1 inch	2.5 cm	
½ Tbsp	8 mL		5 oz	140 g		1¼ inches	3 cm	
1 Tbsp	15 mL		6 oz	170 g		1½ inches	3.5 cm	
1½ Tbsp	23 mL		7 oz	200 g		1¾ inches	4.5 cm	
2 Tbsp	30 mL		8 oz (½ lb)	225 g		2 inches	5 cm	
¼ cup	60 mL		9 oz	255 g		2½ inches	6.5 cm	
⅓ cup	80 mL		10 oz	285 g		3 inches	7.5 cm	
½ cup	125 mL		11 oz	310 g		4 inches	10 cm	
⅔ cup	165 mL		12 oz (¾ lb)	340 g		5 inches	12.5 cm	
¾ cup	185 mL		13 oz	370 g		6 inches	15 cm	
1 cup	250 mL		14 oz	400 g		7 inches	18 cm	
1¼ cups	310 mL		15 oz	425 g		10 inches	25 cm	
1⅓ cups	330 mL		16 oz (1 lb)	450 g		12 inches (1 foot)	30 cm	
1½ cups	375 mL		1¼ lbs	570 g		13 inches	33 cm	
1⅔ cups	415 mL		1½ lbs	670 g		16 inches	41 cm	
1¾ cups	435 mL		2 lbs	900 g		18 inches	46 cm	
2 cups	500 mL		3 lbs	1.4 kg		24 inches (2 feet)	60 cm	
2¼ cups	560 mL		4 lbs	1.8 kg		28 inches	70 cm	
2⅓ cups	580 mL		5 lbs	2.3 kg		30 inches	75 cm	
2½ cups	625 mL		6 lbs	2.7 kg		6 feet	1.8 m	
2¾ cups	690 mL							
3 cups	750 mL							
4 cups / 1 quart	1 L							
5 cups	1.25 L							
6 cups	1.5 L							
7 cups	1.75 L							
8 cups	2 L							
12 cups	3 L							

Liquid measures (for alcohol)

Imperial	Metric
½ fl oz	15 mL
1 fl oz	30 mL
2 fl oz	60 mL
3 fl oz	90 mL
4 fl oz	120 mL

Cans and jars

Imperial	Metric
6 oz	170 mL
14 oz	398 mL
19 oz	540 mL
28 oz	796 mL

Baking pans

Imperial	Metric
5- × 9-inch loaf pan	2 L loaf pan
9- × 13-inch cake pan	4 L cake pan
11- × 17-inch baking sheet	30 × 45 cm baking sheet

Temperature

Imperial	Metric
90°F	32°C
120°F	49°C
125°F	52°C
130°F	54°C
140°F	60°C
150°F	66°C
155°F	68°C
160°F	71°C
165°F	74°C
170°F	77°C
175°F	80°C
180°F	82°C
190°F	88°C
200°F	93°C
240°F	116°C
250°F	121°C
300°F	149°C
325°F	163°C
350°F	177°C
360°F	182°C
375°F	191°C

Oven temperature

Imperial	Metric
200°F	95°C
250°F	120°C
275°F	135°C
300°F	150°C
325°F	160°C
350°F	180°C
375°F	190°C
400°F	200°C
425°F	220°C
450°F	230°C
500°F	260°C
550°F	290°C

ACKNOWLEDGMENTS

While writing this book I often thought about the expression "This is isn't my first rodeo," usually uttered by someone whose experience and jaded know-how allows for the freedom to be cavalier. Because I felt that this was, and is forever solidified as, *my first rodeo*. I had no idea what to expect about this process and how much persistence, charm, and grind would go into a project of this scale.

None of this book would have been possible without the help and support of friends and colleagues, for whom I am endlessly grateful. First I want to thank the chefs, owners, and publicists who believed in the project from day one and worked diligently to get us all the pieces we needed and made sure everyone was on time and on the same page (literally!). To the PR gurus of Miami who wrangled their chefs and were instrumental in making this happen—Larry Carrino, Vanessa Menkes, Ashley Jimenez, and Tara Gilani—rock stars you are. Danny Diaz and Erin Lavan, you championed my efforts and freely shared contacts that helped make this book the success it has become. To Adeena Sussman, for writing the most eloquent and flattering foreword I could ever ask for and for being my mentor and "Sobe wifey"—I cherish our moments together.

This book would also not have been possible without the help and encouragement of my editor, Michelle Meade, and the entire team at Figure 1 whose patience, guidance, and availability helped shepherd me through this often-daunting process.

To the visuals dream team who made the photo shoot a joy to experience, I salute you. Photographer Michael Pisarri, I'm in awe of your ability to coax story from shadow and light. Prop stylist Jocelyn Negron kept things looking detailed and beautiful and art director Naomi MacDougall captured the color and feel of Miami with brilliant vision. You all brought this cookbook to life!

And lastly to the chefs and bartenders who willingly gave their time and their recipes and shared their stories, I am indebted to your talents and accomplishments. I hope my words do justice to the commendable work that you do day in and day out to feed people and create beautiful food and drink.

INDEX

*Page numbers in italics
refer to photos.*

agave oil, 128
AIOLI. *See also* mayo
   chile-vinaigrette, 34
   chipotle, 55
   garlic, 58
aji amarillo sauce, 62.
         See also huancaina sauce,
         cauliflower with
aji panca marinade, 62
ajo blanco, 171
ALMOND(S)
   in cobia with Cara Cara orange, 125
   crispy spiced prawns with, 84
   flour, in ajo blanco, 171
   flour, in coconut crumble, 63
   paste (marzipan), in orgeat
      syrup, 167
ANCHOVY
   in Caesar dressing, 136
   paste, in leche de tigre
      bachiche, 116
anticuchos, lamb, with baby potatoes
   and chile sauce, *61, 62*
ARUGULA
   in carne salata e rucola, 168
   in lemon-saffron linguine, 44–45
   micro, in Chilean sea bass with
      brown butter–soy sauce, 95
   in spaghetti aux fruits de mer, 133
Asian pear, crispy spiced prawns
   with, 84
Aussie lamb anticuchos with baby
   potatoes and chile sauce, *61, 62*
AVOCADO. *See also* guacamole, for
         duck carnitas tacos
   in ceviche, 38
   pico, 21
   pizza, *127,* 128
   purée, 103
   remoulade, 171
   in sexy salad, 132

bachiche, tiradito, 116, *117*
bacon vinaigrette, 32
bamboo shoots, in Thai green
   curry, 89
banana slices, chocolate
   namelaka with, 63
BASIL
   in brown butter–soy sauce, 95
   in charred Romanesco, 92
   in garlic aioli, 58
   in infused watermelon, 34
   in orzo seafood paella, 76
   in pizza mortazza, 150
   in shrimp cakes, 58
   Thai, in Florida red snapper, 113
   Thai, in pho bo, 140–41
   Thai, in Thai green curry, 89
bastani (Persian gelato), 81
beansprouts, in pho bo, 140–41
béchamel sauce, 27
BEEF
   bone-marrow butter, 66
   in carne salata e rucola, 168
   oxtail stew, Cuban-style, 71
   in pho bo, 140–41
   rib-eye steak, crab-crusted, 146, *147*
   short rib ragout, cornbread with,
      65, 66–67
   tartare, 47
BEET
   causa, 115
   emulsion, 121
   in mamey gazpacho, 24
   tartare salad, *119,* 121
BELL PEPPERS
   green, in ceviche, 38
   green, in curry paste, 89
   green, in epis (Haitian seasoning
      base), 19
   green, in oxtail stew, 71
   multicolored, in Thai green curry, 89
   red, in avocado pico, 21
   red, in crab-crusted
      rib-eye steak, 146
   red, in epis (Haitian seasoning
      base), 19

red, in mamey gazpacho, 24
red, in oxtail stew, 71
red, in sambal sauce, 103
red, roasted, in harissa, 92
yellow, in epis (Haitian seasoning
   base), 19
black garlic purée, in
   Chilean sea bass, 95
blood oranges, in cobia with Cara
   Cara orange, 125
bok choy, in Chilean sea bass with
   brown butter–soy sauce, 95
bone-marrow butter, 66
BOTTARGA
   in lemon-saffron linguine, 44–45
   spaghetti, 154, *155*
braised radishes, pan-roasted scallops
   with, 172
BREADCRUMBS. *See also* panko
      breadcrumb(s)
   for ham croquetas, 120
   sourdough, for lemon-saffron
      linguine, 44–45
   in sweet creamed corn, 145
BREAD, IN RECIPES. *See also* tortillas
   brioche, caramelized
      strawberry, *28,* 29
   brioche or country bread, for
      Cubano "croque monsieur," 27
   ciabatta, for carne salata e
      rucola, 168
   crostini, for beef tartare, 47
   sourdough croutons, in
      kale Caesar salad, 136
BRIOCHE
   caramelized strawberry, *28,* 29
   for Cubano "croque monsieur," 27
broth, for pho bo, 140–41
BROWN BUTTER
   plantain gnudi with, 23
   –soy sauce, Chilean sea bass with, 95
   yuzu, 106
burrata, in pizza mortazza, 150
BUTTER. *See also* brown butter
   bone-marrow, 66
   miso, 113

BUTTON MUSHROOMS
in Korean braised chicken with
glass noodles, 72
sautéed, 58

CABBAGE
in pikliz, 19
red, in ceviche, 38
red, in kale Caesar salad, 136
Caesar salad, kale, with
crispy pork belly lardons, *135*, 136

CAKE
grilled chocolate, 129
tiramisu, *149*, 151
calamari. *See* squid
cantaloupe, in beet tartare salad, 121

CAPERS
in avocado remoulade, 171
in beet tartare salad, 121
fried, 101
in grilled octopus, 101
in salmoriglio, 47
Cara Cara orange, cobia with, *124*, 125
caramel chicken wings, *139*, 143
caramelized onions, 137
caramelized plantains, 23
caramelized strawberry
brioche, *28*, 29
caramel sauce, for chicken wings, 143
caramel sauce, for grilled chocolate
cake, 129
carne salata e rucola, 168, *169*

CARROT
in fregola, 153
in Korean braised chicken with
glass noodles, 72
in oxtail stew, 71
pickled, 20
in pikliz, 19
and sour cherry stew (*khoresh
havij ba aloo*), 79, 80
casserole, market fish, 158, *159*

CAULIFLOWER. *See also* Romanesco,
charred, with celery leaf
pesto and harissa
cakes, 171
with huancaina sauce, *31*, 32–33
roasted, with goat cheese and
shishito-herb vinaigrette, 110–11

CELERY LEAF
for Florida red snapper, 113
pesto, charred Romanesco with, 92
ceviche, SoFla fish, *37*, 38
charred Romanesco with celery leaf
pesto and harissa, *91*, 92

CHEESE. *See also* cotija cheese; feta
cheese; Gruyère; Parmesan;
queso añejo; ricotta
burrata, in pizza mortazza, 150
Emmentaler, in Gruyère popovers,
123
fontina, in Gruyère popovers, 123
goat cheese, roasted cauliflower
with, 110–11

mascarpone, in tiramisu, 151
mozzarella, in pizza mortazza, 150
Pecorino Romano, in beef
tartare, 47
queso fresco, in cauliflower with
huancaina sauce, 32–33
Swiss, in Cubano "croque
monsieur," 27
cherry, sour, and carrot stew
(*khoresh havij ba aloo*), 79, 80
chervil, in herb salad, 67

CHICKEN
crispy orange, *83*, 85
Korean braised, with
glass noodles, 72, *73*
wings, caramel, *139*, 143
Chilean mussels, 163
Chilean sea bass with brown
butter–soy sauce, 95
chile(s). *See also* chili flakes; peppers
sauce, lamb anticuchos with, 62
-vinaigrette aioli, 34

CHILI FLAKES
in fregoletta, 153
in havij spice mix, 80
in lemon-saffron linguine, 44–45
in salmoriglio, 47
in sambal sauce, 103
in spaghetti aux fruits de mer, 133
in spaghetti bottarga, 155
in spaghetti with lobster, 49
in spicy lime mayo, 132
chili-mayo sauce, 84

CHIPOTLE
aioli, 55
in duck carnitas, 52
in spicy tahini, 20
chive emulsion, 121

CHOCOLATE. *See also* cocoa powder
cake, grilled, 129
namelaka, 63
chorizo, in Chilean mussels, 163
ciabatta, for carne salata
e rucola, 168

CILANTRO
in avocado pizza, 128
in avocado purée,103
in ceviche, 38
in citric salsa verde, 158
-coconut sauce, 34
in curry paste, 89
in duck carnitas tacos, 52–53
hamachi rolls, 96, *97*
-mango onions, 20–21
in mango pico de gallo, 39
in pho bo, 141–42
in serrano salsa, 53
citric salsa verde, 158

CLAM(S)
in fregoletta, 153
juice, in orzo seafood paella, 76
juice, in sauce, for garlic
shrimp, 165
in lemon-saffron linguine, 44–45

in seafood risotto, 59
in spaghetti aux fruits de mer, 133

COBIA
with Cara Cara orange, *124*, 125
in tiradito bachiche, 116

COCKTAILS
Esotico Rum Cup, 167
Golden Geisha, 107
Jim's Yellow Fedora, *91*, 93
Rum Cake Mai Tai, 69

COCOA POWDER
in grilled chocolate cake, 129
in tiramisu, 151

COCONUT
-cilantro sauce, 34
crumble, chocolate namelaka
with, 63
milk, in ajo blanco, 171
milk, in Thai green curry, 89

COFFEE
in short ribs, 66
in tiramisu, 151

CONDIMENTS. *See also* dressings
and vinaigrettes; marinade;
sauces and spreads
agave oil, 128
avocado pico, 21
curry paste, 89
harissa, 92
mango pico de gallo, 39
salmoriglio, 47

CORN. *See also* tortillas
-bread with short rib ragout,
65, 66–67
Mexican street (*esquites*), 55
sweet creamed, 145
corn tortillas. *See* tortillas

COTIJA CHEESE
for duck carnitas tacos, 52–53
for Mexican street corn
(*esquites*), 55
coulis, tomato, 58
couscous, m'hamsa, and
harissa-spiced lamb, 42–43

CRAB
-crusted rib-eye steak, 146, *147*
imitation, in sexy salad, 132
in sexy salad, 132

CRACKERS
lavash, for m'hamsa couscous,
and harissa-spiced lamb,
42–43
squid ink or shrimp, for
tiradito bachiche, 116
creamed corn, sweet, 145
crepes, lemon soufflé, 77
crisps, potato, 35
crispy orange chicken, *83*, 85
crispy pork belly lardons,
kale Caesar salad with, *135*, 136
crispy spiced prawns with
Asian pear and almonds, *83*, 84
"croque monsieur," Cubano, 27
croquetas, ham, *119*, 120

croutons, sourdough, in kale
Caesar salad, 136
Cuban mayo, 27
Cubano "croque monsieur," 27
Cuban-style oxtail stew, 71
Cuban-style pork roast, 27
CUCUMBER
in Chilean sea bass with brown
butter–soy sauce, 95
in crispy spiced prawns with
Asian pear and almonds, 84
-poblano zhug, 20
in sexy salad, 132
in tuna tartare, 103
in yogurt sauce, 43
culantro leaves, in shishito-herb
vinaigrette, 110
curry, Thai green, 88, 89

Dan's #9, 167
DEMI-GLACE
in Chilean sea bass, 95
in red wine jus, 67
dough, pizza, 128, 150
DRESSINGS AND VINAIGRETTES.
See also condiments; marinade;
sauces and spreads
bacon vinaigrette, 32
Caesar dressing, 136
chile-vinaigrette aioli, 34
dressing for pikliz, 19
shallot vinaigrette, 67
shishito-herb vinaigrette, 110
drinks. See cocktails
duck carnitas tacos, 51, 52–53

EGGPLANT
and harissa-spiced lamb, 42–43
Thai, in Thai green curry, 89
eggs, quail, for beef tartare, 47
Emmentaler, in Gruyère popovers, 123
epis (Haitian seasoning base), 19
Esotico Rum Cup, 167
esquites (Mexican street corn), 55

FENNEL
in Chilean mussels, 163
in kale Caesar salad, 136
in lemon-saffron linguine, 44–45
FETA CHEESE
in charred Romanesco, 92
for mamey gazpacho, 24
FISH. See also anchovy; cobia;
grouper; snapper; yellowtail
Chilean sea bass with brown
butter–soy sauce, 95
casserole, 158, 159
ceviche, 37, 38
fried, and fixins, 20–21
imitation crab, in sexy salad, 132
tacos, 37, 39. See also whole
fried fish and fixins
tiradito bachiche, 116, 117
tuna tartare, 103

flor de papa, 115
Florida fish tacos, 37, 39
Florida red snapper, 112, 113
fontina, in Gruyère popovers, 123
fregoletta, 153
French onion risotto, 137
FRESNO PEPPER
in bacon vinaigrette, 32
in chile-vinaigrette aioli, 34
fried capers, 101
fried fish and fixins, 20–21
frisée, in herb salad, 67

galangal, in curry paste, 89
GARLIC
aioli, 58
black, purée, in Chilean
sea bass, 95
shrimp, 164, 165
gazpacho, mamey, 24, 25
gelato, Persian (bastani), 81
GINGER
in ajo blanco, 171
candied, in coconut-cilantro
sauce, 34
in caramel sauce, 143
in citric salsa verde, 158
in Dan's #9, 167
in marinade, for Korean
braised chicken, 72
in pho bo, 140–41
pickled, for hamachi
cilantro rolls, 96
in roasted cauliflower, 111
in short ribs, 66
glass noodles, braised chicken
with, 72, 73
glazed eggplant, 42
gnudi, plantain, with toasted
hazelnuts and brown butter, 23
goat cheese, roasted cauliflower
with, 110–11
Golden Geisha, 107
granite, passionfruit, chocolate
namelaka with, 63
green bell peppers.
See under bell peppers
green curry, Thai, 88, 89
grilled chocolate cake, 129
grilled octopus, 100, 101
grilled snapper with tamarind
sauce, 87
grilled vegetables, for market
fish casserole, 158
griot and pikliz, 18, 19
GROUPER
for fish tacos, 39
marinated, 38
GRUYÈRE
in béchamel sauce, 27
in French onion risotto, 137
popovers, 123
guacamole, for duck carnitas
tacos, 52–53

guiltless lemon soufflé crepes, 77

habanero pepper, in dressing, for
pikliz, 19
Haitian seasoning base (epis), 19
HAMACHI (YELLOWTAIL)
cilantro rolls, 96, 97
in market fish casserole, 158
ham croquetas, 119, 120
HARISSA, 92
charred Romanesco with, 92
-spiced lamb, eggplant, and
m'hamsa couscous, 41, 42–43
spice mix, 42
havij spice mix, 80
hazelnuts, plantain gnudi with, 23
hearts of palm, 35
HERB(S). See also specific herbs
salad, 67
salad, for Florida red snapper, 113
for sautéed mushrooms, 58
-shishito vinaigrette, 110
huancaina sauce, cauliflower with, 31,
32–33

ice cream, Persian gelato (bastani), 81
imitation crab, in sexy salad, 132
infused watermelon, 34

JALAPEÑO
in bacon vinaigrette, 32
in ceviche, 38
in chile-vinaigrette aioli, 34
in coconut-cilantro sauce, 34
in curry paste, 89
in harissa, 92
in mango pico de gallo, 39
in pho bo, 140–41
pickled, in shishito-herb
vinaigrette, 110
in ricotta cream, 128
Jim's Yellow Fedora, 91, 93

kale Caesar salad with crispy
pork belly lardons, 135, 136
kataifi dough, in cauliflower cakes, 171
khoresh havij ba aloo (Persian carrot
and sour cherry stew), 79, 80
Korean braised chicken with
glass noodles, 72, 73

ladolemono sauce, 101
ladyfingers, in tiramisu, 151
LAMB
anticuchos with baby
potatoes and chile sauce,
61, 62
harissa-spiced, 42–43
lardons, crispy pork belly, kale
Caesar salad with, 135, 136
lavash crackers, for harissa-spiced
lamb and m'hamsa couscous,
42–43
leche de tigre bachiche, 116

LEMON
in beet causa, 115
brown butter, plantain gnudi
with, 23
in Caesar dressing, 136
in carne salata e rucola, 168
in cauliflower cakes, 171
in celery leaf pesto, 92
in charred Romanesco, 92
in citric salsa verde, 158
in cobia with Cara Cara orange, 125
in coconut-cilantro sauce, 34
in dressing, for pikliz, 19
in eggplant purée, 42
in epis (Haitian seasoning base), 19
in garlic shrimp, 165
in Golden Geisha, 107
in infused watermelon, 34
in Jim's Yellow Fedora, 93
in ladolemono sauce, 101
Meyer, in bone-marrow butter, 66
mousse, 161
in orzo seafood paella, 76
in pork roast marinade, 27
in ricotta cream, 128
in Rum Cake Mai Tai, 69
-saffron linguine, 44–45
soufflé crepes, 77
in spaghetti bottarga, 155
vinaigrette, in Florida red
snapper, 113
in yogurt sauce, 43
LEMONGRASS
in caramel sauce, 143
in curry paste, 89
in tamarind sauce, 87
lettuce, for whole fried fish
and fixins, 20–21
LIME
in aji amarillo sauce, 62
in avocado pico, 21
in avocado pizza, 128
in avocado purée, 103
in caramel sauce, 143
in ceviche, 38
in coconut-cilantro sauce, 34
in dressing, for pikliz, 19
in Esotico Rum Cup, 167
in infused watermelon, 34
in leche de tigre bachiche, 116
in mango-cilantro onions, 20–21
in mango pico de gallo, 39
in Mexican street corn
(esquites), 55
in pho bo, 140–41
in pork roast marinade, 27
in salsa rosada, 39
linguine, lemon-saffron, 44–45
LOBSTER
Maine, 105, 106
in orzo seafood paella, 76
in sexy salad, 132
spaghetti with, 48, 49

mahi mahi, for fish tacos, 39
Maine lobster, 105, 106
Mai Tai, Rum Cake, 69
mamey gazpacho, 24, 25
MANGO
-cilantro onions, 20–21
pico de gallo, 39
in sexy salad, 132
MARINADE
aji panca, 62
for Korean braised chicken, 72
pork roast, 27
marinated fish, for ceviche, 38
market fish casserole, 158, 159
mascarpone, in tiramisu, 151
MAYO. See also aioli
-chili sauce, 84
Cuban, 27
spicy lime, 132
Mexican street corn (esquites), 55
m'hamsa couscous, and harissa-
spiced lamb, 42–43
MINT
in chili-mayo sauce, 84
in Esotico Rum Cup, 167
in Florida red snapper, 113
in harissa-spiced lamb, 42
in Jim's Yellow Fedora, 91, 93
in poblano-cucumber zhug, 20
in shishito-herb vinaigrette, 110
in strawberry salad, 29
in yogurt sauce, 43
miso butter, 113
mortadella with pistachio,
in pizza mortazza, 150
mortazza, pizza, 150
mousse, lemon, 161
mozzarella, in pizza mortazza, 150
mullet bottarga. See bottarga
MUSHROOMS
button, in Korean braised chicken
with glass noodles, 72
button, sautéed, 58
shiitake, in Chilean sea bass with
brown butter–soy sauce, 95
shiitake, in short ribs, 66
MUSSELS
Chilean, 163
in orzo seafood paella, 76
in seafood risotto, 59
in spaghetti aux fruits de mer, 133
myoga, in roasted cauliflower, 111

NOODLES. See also pasta
glass, braised chicken with, 72, 73
in pho bo, 140–41
nori, for hamachi cilantro rolls, 96
nuts. See almond(s); hazelnuts,
plantain gnudi with; peanuts, in
spicy tahini; pecans, candied,
for Rum Cake Mai Tai; pistachio
nuts

OCTOPUS
grilled, 100, 101
Spanish, 34–35
OLIVES
black, in salmoriglio, 47
Cerignola, in cobia with Cara Cara
orange, 125
kalamata, in tuna tartare, 103
ONION(S)
caramelized, 137
mango-cilantro, 20–21
risotto, French, 137
ORANGE
blood, in cobia with
Cara Cara orange, 125
Cara Cara, cobia with, 124, 125
in carne salata e rucola, 168
chicken, 83, 85
in dressing, for pikliz, 19
in duck carnitas, 52
navel, in cobia with Cara Cara
orange, 125
in poblano-cucumber zhug, 20
in pork roast marinade, 27
sauce, 85
orange blossom water, in orgeat
syrup, 167
Orelys chocolate namelaka with
coconut crumble, passionfruit
granite, and banana slices, 63
orgeat syrup, 167
in Rum Cake Mai Tai, 69
orzo seafood paella, 75, 76
oxtail stew, Cuban-style, 71

paella, orzo seafood, 75, 76
PANKO BREADCRUMB(S).
See also breadcrumbs
–breaded fish, 39
in crab-crusted rib-eye steak, 146
for shrimp cakes, 58
pan-roasted scallops with parsnip
purée and braised radishes,
172, 173
PARMESAN
in Caesar dressing, 136
in celery leaf pesto, 92
cream, 128
in French onion risotto, 137
in huancaina sauce, 32
in kale Caesar salad, 136
in plantain gnudi, 23
PARSLEY
in celery leaf pesto, 92
in citric salsa verde, 158
in epis (Haitian seasoning base), 19
in grilled octopus, 101
in herb salad, 67
in poblano-cucumber zhug, 20
parsnip purée, pan-roasted
scallops with, 172
passata, in pizza mortazza, 150
passionfruit granite, chocolate
namelaka with, 63

PASTA
fregoletta, 153
gnudi, plantain, with toasted
hazelnuts and brown butter, 23
linguine, lemon-saffron, 44–45
m'hamsa couscous, and harissa-
spiced lamb, 42–43
orzo seafood paella, 75, 76
spaghetti aux fruits de mer, 131, 133
spaghetti bottarga, 154, 155
spaghetti with lobster, 48, 49
pastry cream, for caramelized
strawberry brioche, 29
peanuts, in spicy tahini, 20
PEAR
Asian, crispy spiced prawns with, 84
in marinade, for Korean braised
chicken, 72
PEA SHOOTS
for hamachi cilantro rolls, 96
in herb salad, 67
peas, sugar snap, in grilled vegetables,
158
pecans, candied, for Rum Cake
Mai Tai, 69
Pecorino Romano, in beef tartare, 47
pepitas, in celery leaf pesto, 92
PEPPERS. See also bell peppers;
chile(s); chili flakes; chipotle;
Fresno pepper; jalapeño; red
chiles; serrano chile pepper
habanero pepper, in dressing,
for pikliz, 19
piquillo, in harissa, 92
poblano-cucumber zhug, 20
Scotch bonnet pepper, in dressing,
for pikliz, 19
shishito-herb vinaigrette, 110
Persian carrot and sour cherry stew
(khoresh havij ba aloo), 79, 80
Persian gelato (bastani), 81
pho bo, 139, 140–41
pickled carrots, 20
PICO DE GALLO
avocado, 21
mango, 39
pikliz and griot, 18, 19
piquillo peppers, in harissa, 92
PISTACHIO NUTS
mortadella with, in pizza
mortazza, 150
in Persian gelato (bastani), 81
pita chips, for tuna tartare, 103
PIZZA
avocado, 127, 128
dough, 128, 150
mortazza, 150
plantain gnudi with toasted hazelnuts
and brown butter, 23
poblano-cucumber zhug, 20
ponzu dressing, in Florida red
snapper, 113
popovers, Gruyère, 123
PORK
bacon vinaigrette, 32

belly lardons, kale Caesar salad
with, 135, 136
chorizo, in Chilean mussels, 163
in griot and pikliz, 19
ham croquetas, 119, 120
mortadella with pistachio,
in pizza mortazza, 150
roast, Cuban-style, 27
POTATO(ES)
in beet causa, 115
crisps, 35
hash browns, in fish tacos, 39
in Korean braised chicken with
glass noodles, 72
lamb anticuchos with, 62
in Thai green curry, 89
prawns. See shrimp

quail egg yolks, for beef tartare, 47
QUESO AÑEJO
for duck carnitas tacos, 52–53
for Mexican street corn
(esquites), 55
queso fresco, in cauliflower with
huancaina sauce, 32–33

radicchio, in cobia with
Cara Cara orange, 125
RADISHES
braised, pan-roasted scallops
with, 172
in Chilean sea bass with brown
butter–soy sauce, 95
in Florida red snapper, 113
ragout, short rib, 66–67
RASPBERRIES
in Golden Geisha, 107
in lemon mousse, 161
in lemon soufflé crepes, 77
red bell peppers.
See under bell peppers
RED CHILES
dried, in Korean braised chicken
with glass noodles, 72
dried Thai, in infused watermelon,
34
Thai, in caramel sauce, 143
Thai, in grilled snapper, 87
Thai, in tamarind sauce, 87
red wine jus, 66
rib-eye steak, crab-crusted, 146, 147
RICE
French onion risotto, 137
seafood risotto, 59
sushi, for hamachi cilantro rolls, 96
RICOTTA
cream, 128
in plantain gnudi, 23
RISOTTO
French onion, 137
seafood, 59
roasted cauliflower with goat cheese
and shishito-herb vinaigrette, 110–11
roe, mullet. See bottarga

Romanesco, charred, with celery leaf
pesto and harissa, 91, 92
ROSEWATER
in orgeat syrup, 167
in Persian gelato (bastani), 81
RUM
Cake Mai Tai, 69
Cup, Esotico, 167

SAFFRON
in fregoletta, 153
-lemon linguine, 44–45
in orzo seafood paella, 76
in Persian gelato (bastani), 81
in seafood risotto, 59
in spaghetti with lobster, 49
SALAD. See also salad greens
beet tartare, 119, 121
herb, 67
kale Caesar, with crispy pork belly
lardons, 135, 136
Mexican street corn (esquites), 55
sexy, 131, 132
strawberry, 29
sunchokes tartare, 115
SALAD GREENS. See also specific
salad greens
for cauliflower cakes, 171
for Persian carrot and sour cherry
stew (khoresh havij ba aloo),
79, 80
salmoriglio, 47
SALSA
rosada, 39
serrano, 53
verde, citric, 158
sambal sauce, 103
sandwich, Cubano "croque
monsieur," 27
SAUCES AND SPREADS. See also
condiments; dressings and
vinaigrettes; marinade
aji amarillo sauce, 62
ajo blanco, 171
avocado purée, 103
avocado remoulade, 171
béchamel sauce, 27
beet emulsion, 121
bone-marrow butter, 66
caramel sauce, 129, 143
celery leaf pesto, 92
chile-vinaigrette aioli, 34
chili-mayo sauce, 84
chipotle aioli, 55
chive emulsion, 121
citric salsa verde, 158
coconut-cilantro sauce, 34
Cuban mayo, 27
eggplant purée, 42
feta cream, 24
garlic aioli, 58
huancaina sauce, 32
ladolemono sauce, 101
leche de tigre bachiche, 116

lemon brown butter, 23
miso butter, 113
orange sauce, 85
Parmesan cream, 116
parsnip purée, 172
poblano-cucumber zhug, 20
red wine jus, 66
ricotta cream, 128
salsa rosada, 39
sambal sauce, 103
sauce, for garlic shrimp, 165
serrano salsa, 53
spicy tahini, 20
strawberry sauce, 29
tamarind sauce, 87
tomato coulis, 58
yogurt sauce, 43
yuzu brown butter, 106
sautéed mushrooms, 58
SCALLOPS
    in orzo seafood paella, 76
    with parsnip purée and braised
        radishes, 172, *173*
    in seafood risotto, 59
Scotch bonnet pepper, in dressing,
    for pikliz, 19
sea bass with brown butter–soy
    sauce, 95
SEAFOOD. *See also specific fish
        and shellfish*
    paella, orzo, 75, 76
    risotto, 59
    spaghetti aux fruits de mer, *131*, 133
SEEDS. *See* nuts; pepitas, in celery leaf
        pesto; sesame seeds
SERRANO CHILE PEPPER
    in avocado pizza, 128
    in ricotta cream, 128
    salsa, 53
SESAME SEEDS. *See also* tahini, spicy
    in caramel sauce, 143
    in crispy orange chicken, 85
    in crispy spiced prawns, 84
    in hamachi cilantro rolls, 96
sexy salad, *131*, 132
shallot vinaigrette, 67
SHIITAKE MUSHROOMS
    in Chilean sea bass with brown
        butter–soy sauce, 95
    in short ribs, 66
shishito-herb vinaigrette, roasted
    cauliflower with, 110–11
SHISO LEAVES
    in Florida red snapper, 113
    in roasted cauliflower, 111
short rib ragout, cornbread with,
    65, 66–67
SHRIMP
    cakes, *57*, 58
    crackers, for tiradito bachiche, 116
    crispy spiced prawns, with Asian
        pear and almonds, *83*, 84
    garlic, *164*, 165
    in orzo seafood paella, 76

in seafood risotto, 59
in sexy salad, 132
in spaghetti aux fruits de mer, 133
SNAPPER
    for fish tacos, 39
    Florida red, *112*, 113
    fried, and fixins, 20–21
    with tamarind sauce, 87
    in tiradito bachiche, 116
SoFla fish ceviche, *37*, 38
soufflé crepes, lemon, 77
SOUP
    mamey gazpacho, 24, *25*
    pho bo, *139*, 140–41
sour cherry and carrot stew
    (*khoresh havij ba aloo*), *79*, 80
soy–brown butter sauce,
    Chilean sea bass with, 95
SPAGHETTI
    aux fruits de mer, *131*, 133
    bottarga, 154, *155*
    with lobster, *48*, 49
Spanish octopus, 34–35
spice mix, havij, 80
spicy lime mayo, 132
spicy tahini, 20
SPINACH
    in curry paste, 89
    in garlic aioli, 58
    in orzo seafood paella, 76
SQUID
    calamari, in orzo seafood paella, 76
    ink crackers, for tiradito bachiche,
        116
    in seafood risotto, 59
steak, crab-crusted rib-eye, 146, *147*
STEW
    Cuban-style oxtail, 71
    Persian carrot and sour cherry
        (*khoresh havij ba aloo*), *79*, 80
strawberry brioche, caramelized,
    28, 29
sudachi juice, in shishito-herb
    vinaigrette, 110
sunchokes tartare, 115
sushi rice, for hamachi cilantro
    rolls, 96
sweet creamed corn, 145
sweet potato starch noodles.
    See glass noodles
Swiss cheese, in Cubano
    "croque monsieur," 27
syrup, orgeat, 167

TACOS
    duck carnitas, *51*, 52–53
    fish, *37*, 39. *See also* whole
        fried fish and fixins
tahini, spicy, 20
tamarind sauce, grilled snapper
    with, 87
tarragon, in cauliflower cakes, 171
TARTARE
    beef, 47

beet, salad, *119*, 121
sunchokes, 115
tuna, 103
THAI BASIL
    in Florida red snapper, 113
    in pho bo, 140–41
    in Thai green curry, 89
Thai chiles. *See under* red chiles
Thai green curry, *88*, 89
THYME
    in epis (Haitian seasoning base), 19
    in fregoletta, 153
    in grilled octopus, 101
tilapia, for fish tacos, 39
tiradito bachiche, 116, *117*
tiramisu, *149*, 151
TOMATILLO
    in avocado pico, 21
    in serrano salsa, 53
TOMATO(ES)
    in ceviche, 38
    cherry, in fregoletta, 153
    cherry, in grilled vegetables, 158
    cherry, in pizza mortazza, 150
    cherry, in spaghetti bottarga, 155
    coulis, 58
    grape, in Chilean mussels, 163
    grape, in garlic shrimp, 165
    grape, in spaghetti aux fruits de
        mer, 133
    in mango pico de gallo, 39
    in orzo seafood paella, 76
    passata, in pizza mortazza, 150
    paste, in oxtail stew, 71
    Roma, in shrimp cakes, 58
    in seafood risotto, 59
    in spaghetti with lobster, 49
TORTILLAS
    corn, for duck carnitas tacos, 52–53
    corn, for fish tacos, 39
    for whole fried fish and fixins, 20–21
Treviso, in cobia with Cara Cara
    orange, 125
tuna tartare, 103

watercress, in cobia with Cara Cara
    orange, 125
watermelon, infused, 34
whole fried fish and fixins, 20–21

yellow bell peppers. *See under*
    bell peppers
YELLOWTAIL
    hamachi cilantro rolls, 96, *97*
    in market fish casserole, 158
YOGURT
    in feta cream, 24
    sauce, for harissa-spiced lamb, 43
YUZU
    brown butter, 106
    foam base, for cauliflower, 33
    in hamachi cilantro rolls, 96

zhug, poblano-cucumber, 20

ABOUT THE AUTHOR

SARA LISS is a Miami-based freelance writer and lifestyle reporter, who served as a senior food writer at Miami.com for more than ten years. Her work has been published in a wide range of media, including *Condé Nast Traveler, The Miami Herald, Departures, Modern Luxury MIAMI,* and the Associated Press. She also organizes a pop-up dining experience called Saffron Supper Club and spearheads a monthly community picnic in her town of Surfside, Florida, called Friday Beach. *Miami Cooks* is her first book.